# GREENWICH VILLAGE

I0616854

## ANNA ALICE CHAPIN

1ˢᵗ WORLD
LIBRARY
Literary Society

# Greenwich Village

## Anna Alice Chapin

© 1st World Library – Literary Society, 2005
PO Box 2211
Fairfield, IA 52556
www.1stworldlibrary.org
First Edition

LCCN: 2006930758

Softcover ISBN: 1-4218-2166-4
Hardcover ISBN: 1-4218-2066-8
eBook ISBN: 1-4218-2266-0

Purchase *"Greenwich Village"*
as a traditional bound book at:
www.1stWorldLibrary.org/purchase.asp?ISBN=1-4218-2166-4

1st World Library Literary Society is a nonprofit
organization dedicated to promoting literacy by:

- Creating a free internet library accessible from any
  computer worldwide.
- Hosting writing competitions and offering book
  publishing scholarships.

Readers interested in supporting literacy
through sponsorship, donations or
membership please contact:
literacy@1stworldlibrary.org
Check us out at: www.1stworldlibrary.ORG
and start downloading free ebooks today.

***Greenwich Village***
*contributed by Tim, Ed & Rodney*
*in support of*
*1st World Library Literary Society*

To

VINCENT C. PEPPE

WHO FIRST SUGGESTED THE WRITING OF THIS
BOOK, AND WHOSE UNTIRING EFFORTS HAVE
HAD MUCH TO DO WITH THE SUCCESS OF
GREENWICH VILLAGE AS A POPULAR RESIDENCE
SECTION, THIS BOOK IS DEDICATED

# CONTENTS

# A FIRST WORD

"'Tis an awkward thing to play with souls," - and, to my mind, Greenwich Village has a very personal soul that requires very personal and very careful handling. This little foreword is to crave pardon humbly if my touch has not been light, or deft, or sure. There are so many things that I may have left out, so many ways in which I must have erred.

And I want to thank people too, - just here. So many people there are to thank! I cannot simply dismiss the matter with the usual acknowledgment of a list of authorities - to which, by the bye, I have tried to cling as though they were life-buoys in a stormy sea of research!

There are the kindly individuals, - J.H. Henry, Vincent Pepe, William van der Weyde, J.B. Martin, and the rest, - who have so generously placed their own extensive information and collected material at my disposal. And there are the small army of librarians and clerks and secretaries and so on, who have given me unlimited patience and most encouraging personal interest.

And finally, beyond all these, are the Villagers who have taken me in, and made me welcome, and won my heart for all time. Everyone has been so kind that my "thank you" must take in all of Greenwich.

It is said that hospitality, neighbourliness and genuine cordiality are traits of any well-conducted village. Then be sure that our Village in the city is not behind its rustic fellows. For, wherever you stray or wherever you stop within its confines, you will always find the latch-string hung outside.

"Does a bird need to theorise about building its nest, or boast of it when built? All good work is essentially done that way - without hesitation, without difficulty, without boasting.... And now, returning to the broader question, what these arts and labours of life have to teach us of its mystery, this is the first of their lessons - that the more beautiful the art, the more it is essentially the work of people who ... are striving for the fulfilment of a law, and the grasp of a loveliness, which they have not yet attained.... Whenever the arts and labours of life are fulfilled in this spirit of striving against misrule, and doing whatever we have to do, honourably and perfectly, they invariably bring happiness, as much as seems possible to the nature of man."

- JOHN RUSKIN.

Anna Alice Chapin

# CHAPTER I

# THE CHEQUERED HISTORY OF A CITY SQUARE

... I know not whether it is owing to the tenderness of early association, but this portion of New York appears to many persons the most delectable. It has a kind of established repose which is not of frequent occurrence in other quarters of the long, shrill city; it has a riper, richer, more honourable look than any of the upper ramifications of the great longitudinal thoroughfare - the look of having had something of a social history.

- HENRY JAMES (in "Washington Square").

There is little in our busy, modern, progressive city to suggest Father Knickerbocker, with his three-cornered hat and knee-breeches, and his old-world air so homely and so picturesque. Our great streets, hemmed by stone and marble and glittering plate glass, crowded with kaleidoscopic cosmopolitan traffic, ceaselessly resonant with twentieth century activity, do not seem a happy setting for our old-fashioned and beloved presiding shade. Where could he fall a-nodding, to dream himself back into the quaint and gallant days of the past? Where would he smoke his ancient Dutch pipe in peace? One has a mental picture of Father Knickerbocker shaking his queued head over so much noise and haste, so many new-fangled, cluttering things and ways, such a confusion of aims and pursuits on his fine old island! And he would be a wretched ghost indeed if doomed to haunt only upper New York. But it happens that he has a sanctuary, a haven after his own heart, where he can still draw a breath of relief, among buildings small but full of age and dignity and with the look of homes about them; on restful, crooked little streets where there remain trees and grass-plots; in the old-time purlieus of Washington Square and Greenwich Village!

The history of old New York reads like a romance. There is scarcely a plot of ground below Fourteenth Street without its story and its associations, its motley company of memories and spectres both good and bad, its imperishably adventurous savour of the past, imprisoned in the dry prose of registries and records. Let us just take a glance, a bird's-eye view as it were, of that region which we now know as Washington Square, as it was when the city of New York bought it for a Potter's Field.

Perhaps you have tried to visualise old New York as hard as I have tried. But I will wager that, like myself, you have been unable to conjure up more than a nebulous and tenuous vision, - a modern New York's shadow, the ghostly skeleton of our city as it appears today. For instance, when you have thought of old Washington Square, you have probably thought of it pretty much as it is now, only of course with an old-time atmosphere. The whole Village, with all your best imaginative efforts, persists - does it not? - in being a part of New York proper.

It was not until I had come to browse among the oldest of Manhattan's oldest records, - (and at that they're not very old!) - those which show the reaching out of the fingers of early progress, the first shoots of metropolitan growth, that the picture really came to me. Then I saw New York as a little city which had sprung up almost with the speed of a modern mushroom town. First, in Peter Minuit's day, its centre was the old block house below Bowling Green; then it spread out a bit until it became a real, thriving city, - with its utmost limits at Canal Street! Greenwich and the Bowery Lane were isolated little country hamlets, the only ones on the island, and far, far

Anna Alice Chapin

out of town. They appeared as inaccessible to the urban dwellers of that day as do residents on the Hudson to the confirmed city people nowadays; - nay, still more so, since trains and motors, subways and surface cars, have more or less annihilated distance for us.

Washington Square was then in the real wilds, an uncultivated region, half swamp, half sand, with the Sand Hill Road, - an old Indian trail, - running along the edge of it, and Minetta Creek taking its sparkling course through its centre. It was many years before Minetta was even spanned by a bridge, for no one lived anywhere near it.

Peter Stuyvesant's farm gave the Bowery its name, for you must know that Bouwerie came from the Dutch word *Bouwerij*, which means farm, and this country lane ran through the grounds of the Stuyvesant homestead. A branch road from the Bouwerie Lane led across the stretch of alternate marsh and sand to the tiny settlement of Greenwich, running from east to west. The exact line is lost today, but we know it followed the general limit of Washington Square North. On the east was the Indian trail.

Sarah Comstock says:

"The Indian trail has been, throughout our country, the beginning of the road. In his turn, the Indian often followed the trail of the beast. Such beginnings are indiscernible for the most part, in the dusk of history, but we still trace many an old path that once knew the tread of moccasined feet."

Here, between the short lane that ran from the _Bouwerij_ toward the first young sprout of Greenwich, and the primitive Sand Hill (or Sandy Hill) Trail lay a certain waste tract of land. It was flanked by the sand mounds, - part of the Zantberg, or long range of sand hills, - haunted by wild fowl, and utterly aloof from even that primitive civilisation. The brook flowed from the upper part of the Zantberg Hills to the

Hudson River, and emptied itself into that great channel at a point somewhere near Charlton Street. The name Minetta came from the Dutch root, - *min*, - minute, diminutive. With the popular suffix *tje* (the Dutch could no more resist that than the French can resist *ette*!) it became *Mintje*, - the little one, - to distinguish it from the *Groote Kill* or large creek a mile away. It was also sometimes called *Bestavaar's Killetje*, or Grandfather's Little Creek, but *Mintje* persisted, and soon became Minetta.

Minetta was a fine fishing brook, and the adjacent region was full of wild duck; so, take it all in all, it was a game preserve such as sportsmen love. It seems that the old Dutch settlers were fond of hunting and fishing, for they came here to shoot and angle, as we would go into - let us say - the Adirondacks or the Maine woods!

"A high range of sand hills traversed a part of the island, from Varick and Charlton to Eighth and Green streets," says Mary L. Booth, in her history. "To the north of these lay a valley through which ran a brook, which formed the outlet of the springy marshes of Washington Square...."

And here, on the self-same ground of those "springy marshes," is Washington Square today.

The lonely Zantberg, - the wind-blown range of sand hills; the cries of the wild birds breaking the stillness; the quietly rippling stream winding downward from the higher ground in the north, and now and then, in the spring of the year, overflowing its bed in a wilderness of brambles and rushes; - do these things make you realise more plainly the sylvan remoteness of that part of New York which we now know as Downtown?

A glance at Bernard Ratzer's map - made in the beginning of the last half of the eighteenth century for the English governor, Sir. Henry Moore - shows the only important holdings in the neighbourhood at that time: the Warren place, the Herrin

(Haring or Harring) farm, the Eliot estate, etc. The site of the Square, in fact, was originally composed of two separate tracts and had two sources of title, divided by Minetta Brook, which crossed the land about sixty feet west of where Fifth Avenue starts today. Westward lay that rather small portion of the land which belonged to the huge holdings of Sir. Peter Warren, of whom more anon.

The eastern part was originally the property of the Herrings, Harrings or Herrins, - a family prominent among the early Dutch settlers and later distinguished for patriotic services to the new republic. They appear to have been directly descended from that intrepid Hollander, Jan Hareng of the city of Hoorn, who is said to have held the narrow point of a dike against a thousand Spaniards, and performed other prodigious feats of valour. In the genealogical book I read, it was suggested that the name Hareng originated in some amazingly large herring catch which (I quote verbatim from that learned book) "astonished the city of Hoorn," - and henceforth attached itself to the redoubtable fisherman!

The earliest of the family in this city was one Jan Pietersen Haring, and his descendants worked unceasingly for the liberty of the republic and against the Tory party. In 1748, Elbert Haring received a grant of land which was undoubtedly the farm shown in the Ratzer map. A tract of it was sold by the Harring (Herring) family to Cornelius Roosevelt; it passed next into Jacob Sebor's hands, and in 1795 was bought by Col. William S. Smith, a brilliant officer in Washington's army, and holder of various posts of public office.

There was a Potter's Field, a cemetery for the poor and friendless, far out in the country, - i.e., somewhere near Madison Square, - but it was neither big enough nor accessible enough. In 1789, the city decided to have another one. The tract of land threaded by Minetta Water, half marsh and half sand, was just about what was wanted. It was retired, the right distance from town and excellently adapted to the purposes of a burying ground. The ground, popular historians to the contrary, was by no means uniformly swampy. When filled in, it would, indeed, be dry and sandy, - the sandy soil of Greenwich extends, in some places, to a depth of fifty feet. Accordingly, the city bought the land from the Herrings and made a Potter's Field. Eight years later, by the bye, they bought Colonel Smith's tract too, to add to the field. The entire plot was ninety lots, - eight lots to an acre, - and comprised nearly the entire site of the present square. The extreme western part, a strip extending east of Macdougal Street to the Brook, a scant thirty feet, - was bought from the Warren heirs.

Minetta Lane, which was close by, had a few aristocratic country residents by that time, and everyone was quite outraged by the notion of having a paupers' graveyard so near. Several rich people of the countryside even offered to present the city corporation with a much larger and more valuable plot of ground somewhere else; but the officials were firm. The public notice was relentlessly made, of the purchase of ground "bounded on the road leading from the Bowerie Lane at the two-mile stone to Greenwich."

When you next stroll through the little quiet park in the shadow of the Arch and Turini's great statue of Garibaldi, watching the children at play, the tramps and wayfarers resting, the tired horses drinking from the fountain the S.P.C.A. has placed there for their service and comfort, the old dreaming of the past, and the young dreaming of the future, - see, if you please, if it is not rather a wistfully pleasant thought to recall the poor and the old and the nameless and the humble who were put to rest there a century and a quarter ago?

The Aceldama of the Priests of Jerusalem was "the potter's field to bury strangers in," according to St. Matthew; and in the Syriac version that meant literally "the field of sleep." It is true that when they made use of Judas Iscariot's pieces of silver, they twisted the syllables to mean the "field of blood," but it was a play upon words only. The Field of Sleep was the Potter's Field, where the weary "strangers" rested, at home at last.

There is nothing intrinsically repellent in the memories attached to a Potter's Field, - save, possibly, in this case, a certain scandalous old story of robbing it of its dead for the benefit of the medical students of the town. That was a disgraceful business if you like! But public feeling was so bitter and retributive that the practice was speedily discontinued. So, again, there is nothing to make us recoil, here among the green shadows of the square, from the recollection of the Potter's Field. But there *is* always something fundamentally shocking in any place of public punishment. And, - alas! - there is that stain upon the fair history of this square of which we are writing.

For - there was a gallows in the old Potter's Field. Upon the very spot where you may be watching the sparrows or the budding leaves, offenders were hanged for the edification or intimidation of huge crowds of people. Twenty highwaymen were despatched there, and at least one historian insists that they were all executed at once, and that Lafayette watched the performance. Certainly a score seems rather a large number, even in the days of our stern forefathers; one cannot help wondering if the event were presented to the great Frenchman as a form of entertainment.

In 1795 came one of those constantly recurring epidemics of yellow fever which used to devastate early Manhattan; and in 1797 came a worse one. Many bodies were brought from other burying grounds, and when the scourge of small-pox killed off two thousand persons in one short space, six hundred and sixty-seven of them were laid in this particular public cemetery. During one very bad time, the rich as well as the poor were brought there, and there were nearly two thousand bodies sleeping in the Potter's Field.

People who had died from yellow fever were wrapped in great yellow sheets before they were buried, - a curious touch of symbolism in keeping with the fantastic habit of mind which we find everywhere in the early annals of America. Mr. E.N. Tailer, among others, can recall, many years later, seeing the crumbling yellow folds of shrouds uncovered by breaking coffin walls, when the heavy guns placed in the Square sank too weightily into the ground, and crushed the trench-vaults.

It would be interesting to examine, in fancy, those lost and sometimes non-existent headstones of the Field, - that is, to try to tell a few of the tales that cling about those who were buried there. But the task is difficult, and after all, tombstones yield but cheerless reading. That the sleepers in the Potter's Field very often had not even that shelter of tombstones makes their stories the more elusive and the more melancholy. One or two slight records stand out among the rest, notably the curious one attached to the last of the stones to be removed from Washington Square. I believe that it was in 1857 that Dr. John Francis, in an address before the Historical Society of New York, told this odd story, which must here be only touched upon.

One Benjamin Perkins, "a charlatan believer in mesmeric influence," plied his trade in early Manhattan. He seems to have belonged to that vast army of persons who seriously believe their own teachings even when they know them to be preposterous. Perkins made a specialty of yellow fever, and insisted that he could cure it by hypnotism. That he had a following is in no way strange, considering his day and generation, but the striking point about this is that, when he was exposed to the horror himself, he tried to automesmerise himself out of it. After three days he died, as Dr. Francis says, "a victim of his own temerity."

And still the gallows stood on the Field of Sleep, and also a big elm tree which sometimes served as the "gallows tree." Naturally, Indians and negroes predominated in the lists of malefactors executed. The redmen were distrusted from the beginning on Manhattan, - and with some basic reason, one must admit; - as for the blacks, they were more severely dealt with than any other class. The rigid laws and restrictions of

Anna Alice Chapin

that day were applied especially rigidly to the slaves. A slave was accounted guilty of heavy crimes on the very lightest sort of evidence, and the penalties imposed seem to us out of all proportion to the acts. Arson, for instance, was a particularly heinous offence - when committed by a negro. The negro riots, which form such an exceedingly black chapter in New York's history, and which horrify our more humane modern standards with ghastly pictures of hangings and burnings at the stake, were often caused by nothing more criminal than incendiarism. One very bad period of this sort of disorder started with a trifling fire in Sir. Peter Warren's house, - the source of which was not discovered, - and later grew to ungovernable proportions through other acts of the same sort.

As late as 1819, a young negro girl named Rose Butler was hanged in our Square before an immense crowd, including many women and young children. Kindly read what the New York *Evening Post* said about it in its issue of July 9th:

> "Rose, a black girl who had been sentenced to be hung for setting fire to a dwelling house, and who was respited for a few days, in the hope that she would disclose some accomplice in her wickedness, was executed yesterday at two o'clock near the Potter's Field."

And in Charles H. Haswell's delightful "Reminiscences," there is one passage which has, for modern ears, rather too Spartan a ring:

> "A leading daily paper referred to her (he speaks of Rose) execution in a paragraph of five lines, without noticing any of the unnecessary and absurd details that are given in the present day in like cases; neither was her dying speech recorded...."

Thomas Janvier declares that she was accused of murder, but all other authorities say that poor Rose's "wickedness" had consisted of lighting a fire under the staircase of her master's house, with, or so it was asserted, "a malicious intent." One sees that it was quite easy to get hanged in those days, - especially if you happened to be a negro! The great elm tree, on a branch of which Rose was hanged, stood intact in the Square until 1890. I am glad it is gone at last!

Old Manhattan was as strictly run as disciplinary measures and rules could contrive and guarantee. The old blue laws were stringently enforced, and the penalty for infringement was usually a sharp one. In the unpublished record of the city clerk we find, next to the item that records Elbert Harring's application for a land-grant, a note to the effect that a "Publick Whipper" had been appointed on the same day, at five pounds quarterly.

Public notices of that time, printed in the current press, remind the reader of some of these aforementioned rules and regulations. We read that "Tapsters are forbid to sell to the Indians," and that "unseasonable night tippling" is also tabooed; likewise drinking after nine in the evening when curfew rings, or "on a Sunday before three o'clock, when divine service shall be over."

I wonder whether little old "Washington Hall" was built too late to come under these regulations? It was a roadhouse of some repute in 1820, and a famous meeting place for celebrities in the sporting world. It was, too, a tavern and coffee house for travellers (its punch was famous!) and the stagecoaches stopped there to change horses. At this moment of writing it is still standing, on the south of Washington Square, - I think number 58, - with other shabby structures of wood, which, for some inscrutable reason, have never been either demolished or improved. Now they are doomed at last, and are to make way for new and grand apartment houses; and so these, among the oldest buildings in Greenwich, drift into the mist of the past.

And in that same part of the Square - in number 59 or 60, it is said - lived one who cannot be omitted from any story of the Potter's Field: Daniel Megie, the city's gravedigger. In 1819 he bought a plot of ground from one John Ireland, and erected a small frame house, where he lived and where he stored the tools of his rather grim trade. For three years he dwelt there, smoothing the resting places in the Field of Sleep; then, in 1823, a new Potter's Field was opened at the point now known as Bryant Park, and the bodies from the lower cemetery were carried there. Megie, apparently, lost his job, sold out to Joseph Dean and disappeared into obscurity. It is interesting to note that he bought his plot in the first place for $500; now it is incorporated in the apartment house site which is estimated at about $250,000!

There is a legend to the effect that Governor Lucius Robinson later occupied this same house, but the writer does not vouch for the fact. The Governor certainly lived somewhere in the vicinity, and his favourite walk was on Amity Street, - why can't we call it that now, instead of the cold and colourless Third Street?

I find that I have said nothing of Monument Lane, - sometimes called Obelisk Lane, - yet it was quite a landmark in its day, as one may gather from the fact that Ratzer thought it important enough to put in his official map. It ran, I think, almost directly along North Washington Square, and, at one point, formed part of the "Inland Road to Greenwich" which was the scene of Revolutionary manoeuvres. Monument Lane was so called because at the end of it (about Fifteenth Street and Eighth Avenue) stood a statue of the much-adored English general, James Wolfe, whose storming of the Heights of Abraham in the Battle of Quebec, and attendant defeat of the Marquis de Montcalm, have made him illustrious in history. After the Revolution, the statue disappeared, and there is no record of its fate.

With the passing of the old Potter's Field, came many changes. Mayor Stephen Allen (later lost on the *Henry Clay*), made signal civic improvements; he levelled, drained and added three and a half acres to the field. In short, it became a valuable tract of ground. Society, driven steadily upward from Bowling

Green, Bond Street, Bleecker and the rest, had commenced to settle down in the country. What had yesterday been rural districts were suburbs today.

In 1806 there were as many as fifteen families in this neighbourhood rich and great enough to have carriages. Colonel Turnbull had an "out of town" house at, approximately, Eighth and Macdougal streets, - a charming cottage, with twenty acres of garden land which today are worth millions. Growing tired of living in the country, he offered to sell his place to his friend, Nehemiah Rogers; but the latter decided against it.

"It is too far out of town!" he declared.

"But you have a carriage!" exclaimed the Colonel. "You can drive in to the city whenever you want to!"

The distance was too great, however, and Mr. Rogers did not buy.

By 1826, however, the tide had carried many persons of wealth out to this neighbourhood, and there were more and more carriages to be seen with each succeeding month. All at once, high iron railings were built about the deserted Potter's Field, - a Potter's Field no longer, - and on June 27th of that year a proclamation was issued:

> "The corporation of the city of New York have been pleased to set apart a piece of ground for a military parade on Fourth Street near Macdougal Street, and have directed it to be called 'Washington Military Parade Ground.' For the purpose of honouring its first occupation as a military parade, Colonel Arcularis will order a detachment from his regiment with field pieces to parade on the ground on the morning of the Fourth of July next. He shall fire a national salute and proclaim the name of the parade ground, with such ceremonies as he shall see fit."

This occasion, an anniversary of American independence, seems to have been a most gorgeous affair, with the Governor, Mayor and other officials present, and a monumental feast to wind up with. The menu included, among other dainties, two oxen roasted whole, two hundred hams ("with a carver at each"), and so many barrels of beer that the chronicler seems not to have had the courage to record the precise number!

1827 seems to have seen a real growth of social life around the Washington Parade Ground. The New York *Gazette* of June 7th advertised "three-story dwellings in Fourth Street, between Thompson and Macdougal streets, for sale. The front and rear of the whole range is to be finished in the same style as the front of the Bowery Theatre, and each to have a grass plot in front with iron railings."

This promise of theatrical architecture seems a curious inducement, but it must have been effective, for many exclusive families came - no, flocked, - to live in the houses!

In 1830 there was a grand celebration there in joint honour of the anniversary of the British evacuation and the crowning of Louis Philippe in France. Everybody sang patriotic French and American airs, sent off fireworks, fired salutes and had a wildly enthusiastic time. Incidentally, there were speeches by ex-President Monroe and the Hon. Samuel Gouveneur. Enoch Crosby, who was the original of Fenimore Cooper's famous *Harvey Birch* in "The Spy," was present, and so was David Williams, one of the captors of Major Andre, - not to mention about thirty thousand others!

This year saw, too, the founding of the University of the City of New York, on the east side of the Square, - or rather, the Parade Ground, as it was then. That fine old educational institution came close to having its cornerstones christened with blood, for it was the occasion of the well-known, - shall we say the notorious? - "Stonecutters' Riots." The builders contracted for work to be done by the convicts of Sing Sing Prison, and the city workmen, or Stonecutters' Guild, - already strong for unions, - objected. In fact, they objected so strenuously that the Twenty-seventh Regiment (now our popular Seventh) was called out, and stayed under arms in the Square for four days and nights; after which the disturbance died down.

The next important labour demonstration in the Square was in 1855, when, during a period of "hard times," eight thousand workmen assembled there with drums and trumpets, and made speeches in the most approved and up-to-date agitator style, collecting a sum of money which went well up into four figures!

In 1833 society folded its wings and settled down with something resembling permanence upon the corner of the "Snug Harbour" lands, which formed the famous North Side of Washington Square. Of all social and architectural centres of New York, Washington Square North has changed least. Progress may come or go, social streams may flow upward with as much speed, energy and ambition as they will; the eddies leave one quiet and lovely pool unstirred. That fine row of stately houses remains the symbol of dignified beauty and distinction and an aristocracy that is not old-fashioned but perennial.

Such names as we read associated with the story of Washington Square and its environs! Names great in politics and patriotism, in art and literature, in learning and distinction, in fashion and fame and architecture. Hardly one of them but is connected with great position or great achievement or both. Rhinelander, Roosevelt, Hamilton, Chauncey, Wetmore, Howland, Suffern, Vanderbilt, Phelps, Winthrop, - the list is too long to permit citing in full. Three mayors have lived there, and in the immediate vicinity dwelt such distinguished literary persons as Bayard Taylor, Henry James, George William Curtis, N.P. Willis (*Nym Crynkle*), our immortal Poe himself, Anne Lynch, - poetess and hostess of one of the first and most distinguished salons of America - Charles Hoffman, editor of the *Knickerbocker*, and so on.

Another centre of wit and wisdom was the house of Dr. Orville Dewey, - whose Unitarian Church, at Broadway and Waverly Place, was the subject of the first successful photograph in this country by the secret process confided to Morse by Daguerre.

Edgar Allan Poe lived with his sick young wife Virginia, on Carmine Street, and lived very uncomfortably, too. The name of his boarding-house keeper is lost to posterity, but the poet wrote of her food: "I wish Kate our cat could see it. She would faint."

Poor Poe lived always somewhere near the Square. Once in a while he moved away for a time, but he invariably gravitated back to it and to his old friends there. It was in Carmine Street that he wrote his "Arthur Gordon Pym," with Gowans the publisher for a fellow lodger; it was on Sixth Avenue and Waverly Place that he created "Ligeia" and "The Fall of the House of Usher." After Virginia's death, he took a room just off the Square, and wrote the "Imp of the Perverse," with her picture (it is said) above his desk. It was at these quarters that Lowell called on him, and found him, alas! "not himself that day." The old Square has no stranger nor sadder shade to haunt it than that of the brilliant and melancholy genius who in life loved it so well.

Poe's friend Willis published many of his stories and articles in the *Sun*, still a newcomer in the old field of journalism. Willis has his own connection with the tale of the Square, though not a very glorious one. The town buzzed for days with talk of the sensational interview between *Nym Crinkle* and Edwin Forrest, the actor. Mr. Willis made some comments on Forrest's divorce, in an editorial, and that player, so well adored by the American public, took him by the coat collar in Washington Square and exercised his stage-trained muscles by giving him a thorough and spectacular thrashing.

Somewhere in that neighbourhood, much earlier, another editor, William Coleman, founder of the *Evening Post*, and

Jeremiah Thompson, Collector of the Port, fought a duel to the death. It was indeed to the death, for Thompson was wounded fatally. But duels were common enough in those days; we feel still the thrill of indignation roused by the shooting of Alexander Hamilton by Burr.

The old University of New York - where Professor Morse conducted his great experiments in telegraphy, where Samuel Colt in his tower workroom perfected his revolver, where the Historical Society of New York was first established and where many of our most distinguished citizens received their education - was never a financial success. For a time they tried to make it pay by taking tenants - young students, and bachelors who wished seclusion for writing or research. Then, in the course of time, it was moved away to the banks of the Hudson. On the site now stands a modern structure, where, to be sure, a few of the old University departments are still conducted, but which is chiefly celebrated as being the first all-bachelor apartment house erected in town. It is appropriately called the "Benedick," after a certain young man who scoffed at matrimony, - and incidentally got married!

And a few of the families stay beneath the roofs their forefathers built, watching, as they watched, the same quiet trees and lawns and paths of the most charming square in all New York: De Forest, Rhinelander, Delano, Stewart, De Rham, Gould, Wynkoop, Tailer, Guinness, Claflin, Booth, Darlington, Gregory, Hoyt, Schell, Shattuck, Weekes, - these, and others are still the names of the residents of Washington Square North. Father Knickerbocker, coming to smoke his pipe here, will be in good company, you perceive!

The recollections of many living persons who recall the old Square and other parts of early New York, bring forcibly to us the realisation of the speed with which this country of ours has evolved itself. In one man's lifetime, New York has grown from a small town just out of its Colonial swaddling clothes to the greatest city in the world. These reminiscences, then, are but memories of yesterday or the day before. We do not have

Anna Alice Chapin

to take them from history books but from the diaries of men and women who are still wide-eyed with wonder at the changes which have come to their city!

"The town was filled with beautiful trees," says one man (who remembers Commodore Vanderbilt, with the splendid horses, the fine manner and the unexampled profane eloquence), "but the pavements were very dirty. Places like St. John's Park and Abingdon Square were quiet and sweet and secluded. Where West Fourth Street and West Eleventh Street met it was so still you could almost hear the grass grow between the cobblestones! Everything near the Square was extremely exclusive and fashionable. Washington and Waverly places were very aristocratic indeed."

Waverly Place, by the bye, got its name through a petition of select booklovers who lived thereabouts and adored Sir. Walter Scott. It speaks well for the good taste of the aristocratic quarter, even though the tribute came a bit late, - about twenty years after "Waverley" was published!

The celebrated north side of the Square was called, by the society people, "The Row," and was, of course, the last word in social prestige. But, for all its lofty place in the veneration of the world and his wife, its ways were enchantingly simple, if we may trust the tales we hear. In the Square stood the "Pump With The Long Handle," and thence was every bucketful of washing water drawn by the gilt-edged servants of the gilt-edged "Row"! The water was, it is said, particularly soft, - rain, doubtless, - and day by day the pails were carried to the main pump to be filled!

When next you look at the motor stages gliding past the Arch, try, just for a moment, to visualise the old stages which ran on Fifth Avenue from Fulton Ferry uptown. They were very elaborate, we are told, and an immense improvement on the old Greenwich stagecoaches, and the great lumbering vehicles that conveyed travellers along the Post Road. These new Fifth Avenue stages were brightly painted: the body of the coach was navy blue, the running gear white, striped with red, and the lettering and decorations of gold. A strap which enabled the driver to open and close the door without descending from his seat was looked upon as an impressive innovation! Inside, there were oil paintings on panels, small candles in glass boxes for illumination, and straw on the floor to keep your feet warm. These luxuries justified the high rate which was charged. The fare was ten cents!

In very heavy snowstorms the stages were apt to get stalled, so that a few stage sleighs were run in midwinter, but only in the city proper. Their farthest uptown terminal was at Fourteenth Street, so they were not much help to suburbanites!

No single article, or chapter, can even attempt to encompass the complete story of Washington Square. Covering the entire period of the city's history, passing through startling changes and transformations, the scene of great happenings, the background of illustrious or curious lives, - it is probably more typical of the vertiginous development of New York than any single section. The Indians, the Dutch, the English, the Colonials, the Revolutionists, the New Americans, the shining lights of art, science, fashion and the state, have all passed through it, confidently and at home. The dead have slept there; wicked men have died there and great ones been honoured. Belles and beaux have minced on their way beneath the thick green branches, - branches that have also quivered to the sound of artillery fire saluting a mighty nation newborn. Nothing that a city can feel or suffer or delight in has escaped Washington Square. Everything of valour and tragedy and gallantry and high hope - that go to making a great town as much and more than its bricks and mortar - are in that nine and three-quarters acres that make up the very heart and soul of New York.

The lovely Arch first designed by Stanford White and erected by William Rhinelander Stewart's public-spirited efforts, on April 30, 1889, was in honour of the centennial anniversary of Washington's inauguration; it was so beautiful that, happily, it was later made permanent in marble, and in all the town there could have been found no more fitting place for it.

In every really great city there is one place which is, in a sense, sacred from the profanation of too utilitarian progress. However commercialised Paris might become, you could not cheapen the environs of Notre Dame! Whatever happens to us, let us hope that we will always keep Washington Square as it is today, - our little and dear bit of fine, concrete history, the one perfect page of our old, immortal New York!

Father Knickerbocker, may you dream well!

## CHAPTER II

## THE GREEN VILLAGE

God tempers the wind to the shorn lamb down Greenwich way!

- THOMAS JANVIER.

Did you know that "Greenwich Village" is tautology? That region known affectionately as "Our Village" is Greenwich, pure and simple, and here is the "why" of that statement.

The word *wich* is derived from the Saxon *wick*, and originally had birth in the Latin *vicus*, which means village. Hence, Greenwich means simply the Green Village, and was evidently a term describing one of the first small country hamlets on Manhattan. Captain Sir. Peter Warren, on whom be peace and benedictions, is usually given the credit of having given Greenwich its name, the historians insisting that it was the name of his own estate, and simply got stretched to take in the surrounding countryside. This seems rather a stupid theory. The Warrens were undoubtedly among the earliest representative residents in the little country resort, but by no stretch of imagination could any private estate, however ample or important, be called a village. But Greenwich was the third name to be applied to this particular locality.

Once upon a time there was a little settlement of Indians - the tribe was called the Sappocanicon or Sappokanikee. Like other redmen they had a gift for picking out good locations for their huts or wigwams - whatever they were in those days. On this island of Manhattan they had appropriated the finest, richest, yet driest piece of ground to be had. There were woods and fields; there was a marvellous trout stream (Minetta Water); there was a game preserve, second to none, presented to them by the Great Spirit (in the vicinity of Washington Square). There was pure air from the river, and a fine loamy soil for their humble crops. It was good medicine.

They adopted it far back in those beginnings of American history of which we know nothing. When you go down to the waterfront to see the ships steam away, you are probably standing where the braves and squaws had their forest home overlooking the river.

But their day passed. Peter Minuit - who really was a worth-while man and deserved to be remembered for something besides his thrifty deal in buying Manhattan for twenty-four dollars - cast an eye over the new territory with a view to developing certain spots for the Dutch West India Company. He staked out the Sappokanican village tentatively, but it was not really appropriated until Wouter Van Twiller succeeded Minuit as director general and Governor of the island.

Van Twiller was not one of the Hollanders' successes. R.R. Wilson says of him, "Bibulous, slow-witted and loose of life and morals, Van Twiller proved wholly unequal to the task in hand." Representing the West India Company, he nevertheless held nefarious commerce with the Indians - it is even reported that he sold them guns and powder in violation of express regulations - and certainly he was first and forever on the make. But before he was removed from office (because of these and other indiscretions) he had founded Our Village, - so may his soul rest in peace!

Not that he intended to do posterity a favour. He never wanted to help anyone but himself. But, in the first year of his disastrous governorship, he got the itch of tobacco speculation. He knew there was money in it.

He, too, looked over the Indian village above the river, and he, too, found it good. He made it the Company's Farm Number 3, but he did not work it for the company. Not he! He worked it for Wouter Van Twiller, as he worked everything else. He eliminated the Indians by degrees, whether by strategy or force history does not say. R.R. Wilson says it was "rum and warfare." Anyway, they departed to parts unknown and Van Twiller built a farm and started an immense tobacco plantation. As the tobacco grew and flourished the place became known by the Dutch as the Bossen Bouwerie - the farm in the woods. It was one of the very earliest white settlements on the whole island. R.R. Wilson says, "Rum and warfare had before this made an end of the Indian village of the first days. Its Dutch successor, however, grew from year to year."

The names of these first Dutch residents of the Bossen Bouwerie - or Sappocanican as it was still occasionally called - are not known, but it is certain that there were a number of them. In the epoch of Peter Stuyvesant someone mentioned the houses at "Sappokanigan," and in 1679, after the British had arrived, a descriptive little entry was made in one of those delightfully detailed journals of an older and more precise generation than ours. The diary was the one kept by the Labadist missionaries - Dankers and Sluyter - and was only recently unearthed by Henry Murphy at The Hague. It runs as follows:

"We crossed over the island, which takes about three-quarters of an hour to do, and came to the North River, which we followed a little within the woods to Sapokanikee. Gerrit having a sister and friends, we rested ourselves and drank some good beer, which refreshed us. We continued along the shore to the city, where we arrived at an early hour in the evening, very much fatigued, having walked this day about forty miles. I must add, in passing through this island we sometimes encountered such a sweet smell in the air that we stood still; because we did not know what it was we were meeting."

It is odd that the Dutch names in Greenwich have died out as much as they have. There is something in Holland blood which has a way of persisting. They - the old Manhattan Dutch anyway - had a certain stubborn individuality of their own, which refused to give way or compromise. I have always felt that the way the Dutch ladies used to drink their tea was a most illuminating sidelight upon their racial characteristics. They served the dish of tea and the sugar separately - the latter in a large and awkward hunk from which they crunched out bites as they needed them. Now I take it that there was no particular reason for this inconvenient and labourious method, except that it was *their way*. They were used to doing things in an original and an unyielding fashion. I believe a real old-world *Mevrouw* would have looked as coldly askance upon the innovation of putting the sugar *in* the tea, as she looked at the pernicious ingress of the devil-endowed Church of England.

In 1664 came the English rule in what had been New Amsterdam and with it British settlers and a new language. So the Bossen Bouwerie became Green Wich (later clipped in pronunciation to *Grinnich*), the Green Village, and a peaceful, remote little settlement it remained for many a long year.

Now came the rich and great in search of country air, health, rest or change of scene. Colonial society was not so different from twentieth century society. They, too, demanded occasional doses of rustic scenery and rest cures; and they began to drift out to the green little hamlet on the Hudson where they could commune with nature and fortify themselves with that incomparable air. Captain Warren, Oliver de Lancey, James Jauncey, William Bayard and Abraham Mortier all acquired estates there. The road to Greenwich was by far the most fashionable of all the Colonial drives.

Greenwich Road ran along the line of our present Greenwich

Street, and gave one a lovely view of the water. At Lispenard's Salt Meadows (Canal Street) it ran upon a causeway, but the marshes overflowed in the spring, and soon they opened another road known as the Inland Road to Greenwich. This second lane ran from the Post Road or Bowery, westward over the fields and passing close to the site of the Potter's Field. This, I understand, was the favourite drive of the fashionable world a century and a half ago.

If anyone wants to really taste the savour of old New York, let him read the journals of those bygone days. Better than any history books will they make the past live again, make it real to you with its odd perfumes, and its stilted mannerisms, and its high-hearted courage and gallantry.

I know of no quainter literature than is to be found in these very old New York papers. The advertisements alone are pregnant with suggestions of the past - colour, atmosphere, the subtle fragrance and flavour of other days. We read that James Anderson of Broadway has just arrived from London "in the brig Betsy" with a load of "the best finished boot legs." Another gentleman urges people to inspect his "crooked tortoise-shell combs for ladies and gentlemen's hair, his vegetable face powder - his nervous essence for the toothache, his bergamot, lemon, lavendar and thyme" - and other commodities.

Sales were advertised of such mixed assortments as the following:

> "For Sale:
> "A negro wench.
> "An elegant chariot.
>
> "Geneva in pipes, cloves, steel, heart and club, scale beams, cotton in bales, Tenerisse wines in pipes, and quarter casks."

In several old papers you find that two camels were to be seen in a certain stable, at a shilling a head for adults and sixpence for children. The camels were a novelty and highly popular.

Take this item, for instance, from the good old *Daily Advertiser*, chronicler of the big and little things of Manhattan's early days. It gives a fine example of old-style journalism. Observe the ingenuity with which a page of narrative is twisted into the first sentence. The last two are the more startling in their abrupt fashion of leaving the reader high and dry. The cow is starred; obviously the man appears a minor actor:

> "On Thursday afternoon, as a man of genteel appearance was passing along Beekman Street, he was attacked by a cow, and notwithstanding his efforts to avoid her, and the means he used to beat her off, we are sorry to say that he was so much injured as to be taken up dead. The cow was afterward killed in William Street. We have not been able to learn the name of the deceased"!!

Some of the items contain genuine if unconscious humour, - such as the record of the question brought up before the City Council: "Whether attorneys are thought useful to plead in courts or not?" Answer: "It is thought not."

Then there is the proclamation that if any Indian was found drunk in any street, and it could not be ascertained where he got the liquor, the whole street was to be fined!

Among the earlier laws duly published in the press was that hogs should not be "suffered to goe or range in any of the streets or lands." In 1684 eight watchmen were appointed at twelve-pence a night. But read them for yourselves, - they are worth the trouble you will have to find them!

There were many queer trades in New York, and all of them, or nearly all, advertised in the daily journals. In column on column of yellowed paper and quaint f-for-s printing, we read exhortations to employ this or that man, most of them included in the picturesque verse whose author I do not know:

> *"Plumbers, founders, dyers, tanners, shavers,*
> *Sweepers, clerks and criers, jewelers, engravers,*
> *Clothiers, drapers, players, cartmen, hatters, nailers,*
> *Gaugers, sealers, weighers, carpenters, and sailors!"*

And read the long-winded, yet really beautiful old obituary notices; the simple news of battles and high deeds; the fiery, yet pedantic, political editorials. Oh, no one knows anything about Father Knickerbocker until he has read the same newspapers that Father Knickerbocker himself read, - when he wasn't writing for them!

The Revolution had passed and Greenwich was a real village, and growing with astonishing rapidity, even in that day of lightning development.

In 1807 they started to do New York over, and they kept at it faithfully and successfully until 1811. Then began the laying out of streets according to numbers and fixed measurements, instead of by picturesque names and erratic cow-path meanderings. Gouverneur Morris, Simeon de Witt and John Rutherford were appointed by the city to take charge of this task, and, as one writer points out, they did not do it as badly as they might have done, nor as we are inclined to think they did when we try to find our way around lower New York today. The truth is that Greenwich had grown up, and always has grown up ever since, in an entirely independent and obstinate fashion all its own. There was not the slightest use in trying to make its twisty curlicue streets conform to any engineering plan on earth; so those sensible old-time folk didn't try. William Bridges, architect and city surveyor, entrusted with the job, mentions "that part of the city which lies south of Greenwich Lane and North Street, and which was not included in the powers vested in the commissioners." And so Our Village remains itself, utterly and arrogantly untouched by the confining orthodoxy of the rest of the town!

Anna Alice Chapin

The passing of the British rule was the signal for variously radical democratic changes, not only in customs and forms, but in nomenclature. After they had melted up a leaden statue of King George and made it into American bullets, they went about abolishing every blessed thing in the city which could remind them of England and English ways. The names of the streets were, of course, nearly all intrinsically English. A few of the old Dutch names persisted - Bleecker, Vandam, and so on - but nearly every part of the town was named for the extolling of Britain and British royalty. Away then, said New York, with the sign manuals of crowns and autocracy!

In 1783, when the English evacuated Manhattan, the *Advertiser* published: "May the remembrance of this DAY be a lesson to princes!" and in this spirit was the last vestige of imperial rule systematically expunged from the city. Crown Street was a red rag to the bull of Young America; it was called Liberty, and thus became innocuous! Queen Street doffed its ermine and became homely and humble, under the name of Cedar. King Street was now Pine. King George Street was abolished altogether, according to the chronicles. One is curious to know what they did with it; it must be difficult to lose a street entirely! A few streets and squares named for individual Englishmen who had been friendly to America were left unmolested - Abingdon Square, and also Chatham Street, which had been given its appellation in honour of the ever popular William Pitt, Earl of Chatham; Chatham Square, indeed, exists to this day.

Greenwich was at all times a resort for those who could afford it, an exclusive and beautiful country region where anyone with a full purse could go to court health and rest among the trees and fields and river breezes. It was destined to become the most popular, flourishing and prosperous little village that ever grew up over night. Those marvellously healthy qualities as to location and air, that fine, sandy soil, made it a haven, indeed, to people who were afraid of sickness. And in those days the island was continually swept by epidemics - violent, far-reaching, and registering alarming mortality. Greenwich seemed to be the only place where one didn't get yellow fever or anything else, and terrorised citizens began to rush out there in droves, not only with their bags and their baggage, and their wives and children, but with their business too!

John Lambert, an English visitor to America in 1807, writes:

> "As soon as yellow fever makes its appearance, the inhabitants shut up their shops and fly from their homes into the country. Those who cannot go far on account of business, remove to Greenwich, situate on the border of the Hudson about two or three miles from town. The banks and other public offices also remove their business to this place and markets are regularly established for the supply of the inhabitants."

Things went so fast for Greenwich during the biggest of the yellow fever "booms" that one old chronicler (whose name I regret not being able to find) declares he "saw the corn growing on the corner of Hammond Street (West Eleventh) on a Saturday morning, and by the next Monday Niblo and Sykes had built a house there for three hundred boarders!"

Devoe says that:

> "The visits of yellow fever in 1798, 1799, 1803 and 1805 tended much to increase the formation of a village near the Spring Street Market and one also near the State Prison; but the fever of 1882 built up many streets with numerous wooden  buildings for the uses of the merchants, banks (from which  Bank Street took its name), offices, etc."

"'The town fairly exploded,'" quotes Macatamney, - from what writer he does not state, - "'and went flying beyond its bonds as though the pestilence had been a burning mine.'"

It was in 1822 that Hardie wrote:

Anna Alice Chapin

"Saturday, the 24th of August our city presented the appearance of a town beseiged. From daybreak till night one line of carts, containing boxes, merchandise and effects, was seen moving towards Greenwich Village and the upper parts of the city. Carriages and hacks, wagons and horsemen, were scouring the streets and filling the roads; personswith anxiety strongly marked on their countenances, and with hurried gait, were hustling through the streets. Temporary stores and offices were erecting, and even on the ensuing day (Sunday) carts were in motion, and the saw and hammer busily at work. Within a few days thereafter the custom house, the post office, the banks, the insurance offices and the printers of newspapers located themselves in the village or in the upper part of Broadway, where they were free from the impending danger; and these places almost instantaneously became the seat of the immense business usually carried on in the great metropolis."

Bank Street got its name in this way, the city banks transferring their business thither literally overnight, ready to do business in the morning.

Miss Euphemia M. Olcott in her delightful recollections of the past in New York, gives us some charming snapshots of a still later Greenwich as she got them from her mother who was born in 1819.

"She often visited in Greenwich Village, both at her grandfather's and at the house of Mr. Abraham Van Nest, which had been built and originally occupied by Sir. Peter Warren. But she never thought of going *so far* for less than a week! [She lived at Fulton and Nassau streets.] There was a city conveyance for part of the way, and then the old Greenwich stage enabled them to complete the long journey. This ran several times a day, and when my mother committed her hymn:

*"'Hasten, sinner, to be wise,*

she told us that for some years it never occurred to her that it could mean anything in the world but the Greenwich stage."

In further quoting her mother, she tells of Sir. Peter's house itself - then Mr. Van Nest's - as a square frame residence, with gardens both of flowers and vegetables, stables and numbers of cows, chickens, pigeons and peacocks. In the huge hall that ran through the house were mahogany tables loaded with silver baskets of fresh-made cake, and attended by negroes.

In our next chapter we are going back to meet this house a bit more intimately, and find out something of those who built it and lived in it, that fine gentleman, Sir. Peter Warren and his beautiful lady, - Susannah.

But let us not forget.

Greenwich was not exclusively a settlement of the rich and great nor even solely a health resort and refuge. There were, besides the fine estates and the mushroom business sections, two humbler off-shoots: Upper and Lower Greenwich. The first was the Skinner Road - now Christopher Street; the second lay at the foot of Brannan Street - now Spring. To the Upper Greenwich in 1796 came a distinction which would seem to have been of doubtful advantage, - the erection of the New York State Prison. It stood on Amos Street, now our Tenth, close to the river and was an imposing structure for its time - two hundred feet in length with big wings, and a stone-wall enclosure twenty feet in height.

Strange to say the Greenwichers did not object to the prison. They were quite proud of it, and seemed to consider it rather as an acquisition than a plague spot. No other village had a State Prison to show to visitors; Greenwich held its head haughtily in consequence.

A hotel keeper in 1811 put this "ad." in the *Columbia*:

"A few gentlemen may be accommodated with board and lodging at this pleasant and healthy situation, a few doors from the State Prison. The Greenwich stage passes from this to the Federal Hall and returns five times a day."

Janvier says that the prison at Greenwich was a "highly volcanic institution." They certainly seemed never out of trouble there. Behind its walls battle, murder and sudden death seemed the milder diversions. Mutiny was a habit, and they had a way of burning up parts of the building when annoyed. On one occasion they shut up all their keepers in one of the wings before setting fire to it, but according to the *Chronicle* "one more humane than the rest released them before it was consumed."

Hugh Macatamney declares that these mutinies were caused by terrible brutality toward the prisoners. It is true that no one was hanged in the jail itself, the Potter's Field being more public and also more convenient, all things considered, but the punishments in this New York Bridewell were severe in the extreme. Those were the days of whippings and the treadmill, - a viciously brutal invention, - of bread and water and dark cells and the rest of the barbarities which society hit upon with such singular perversity as a means of humanising its derelicts. The prison record of Smith, the "revengeful desperado" who spent half a year in solitary confinement, is probably of as mild a punishment as was ever inflicted there.

In the grim history of the penitentiary there is one gleam of humour. Mr. Macatamney tells it so well that we quote his own words:

"A story is told of an inmate of Greenwich Prison who had been sentenced to die on the gallows, but at the last moment, through the influence of the Society of Friends, had his sentence commuted to life imprisonment, and was placed in charge of the shoe shop in the prison. The

Quakers worked for his release, and, having secured it, placed him in a shoe shop of his own. His business flourished, and he was prominently identified with the progress of the times. He had an itching palm, however, and after a time he forged the names of all his business friends, eloped with the daughter of one of his benefactors and disappeared from the earth, apparently. 'Murder will out' A few years after the forger returned to the city, and established himself under an assumed name in the making of shoes, forgetting, however, to maintain compla-cency, and thinking that no one would recognise him. In a passion at what he considered the carelessness of one of his workmen regarding the time some work should have been delivered, he told the man he should not have promised it, as it caused disappointment. 'Master,' said the workman, 'you have disappointed me worse than that.' 'How, you rascal?' 'When I waited a whole hour in the rain to see you hanged.'"

In 1828 and 1829 the prisoners were transferred to Sing Sing, and the site passed into private hands and the Greenwich State Prison was no more. I believe there's a brewery there now.

It is an odd coincidence that the present Jefferson Market Police Court stands now at Tenth Street, - though a good bit further inland than the ancient State's Prison. The old Jefferson Market clock has looked down upon a deal of crime and trouble, but a fair share of goodness and comfort too. It is hopeful to think that the present regime of Justice is a kindlier and a cleaner one than that which prevailed when the treadmill and the dark cell were Virtue's methods of persuading Vice.

Someone, I know not who, wrote this apropos of prisons in Greenwich:

*"In these days fair Greenwich Village*
*Slept by Hudson's rural shores,*
*Then the stage from Greenwich Prison*
*Drove to Wall Street thrice a day -*

Anna Alice Chapin

*Now the sombre 'Black Maria'*
*Oftener drives the other way."*

But I like to think that the old clock, if it could speak, would have some cheering tales to tell. I like to believe that ugly things are slipping farther and farther from Our Village, that honest romance and clean gaiety are rather the rule there than the exception, and that, perhaps, the day will sometime dawn when there will be no more need of the shame of prisons in Greenwich Village.

The early social growth of the city naturally centred about its churches. Even in Colonial days conservative English society in New York assembled on Sunday with a devotion directed not less to fashion than to religion. We must not forget that America was really not America then, but Colonial England. A graceful militarism was the order of the day, and in the fashionable congregations were redcoats in plenty. The Church of England, as represented and upheld by Trinity Parish, was the church where everyone went. If one were stubborn in dissenting - which meant, briefly, if one were Dutch - one attended such of those sturdy outposts of Presbyterianism as one could find outside the social pale. But one was looked down upon accordingly.

It is not hard to make for oneself a colourful picture of a typical Sunday congregation in these dead and gone days. Trinity was the Spiritual Headquarters, one understands; St. Paul's came later, and was immensely fashionable. Though it was rather far out from Greenwich the Greenwich denizens patronised it at the expense of time and trouble. A writer, whose name I cannot fix at the moment, has described the Sabbath attendance: - ladies in powder and patches alighting from their chaises; servants, black of skin and radiant of garment; officers in scarlet and white uniforms (Colonel "Ol" de Lancey lost his patrimony a bit later because he clung to his!) - a soft, fluttering, mincing crowd - most representative of the Colonies, and loathed by the stiff-necked Dutch.

Trinity got its foothold in 1697, and the rest of the English churches had holdings under the Trinity shadow. St. Paul's (where Sir. Peter Warren paid handsomely for a pew, and which is today perhaps the oldest ecclesiastic edifice in the city, and certainly the oldest of the Trinity structures) was built in 1764, on the street called Vesey because of the Rev. Mr. Vesey, its spiritual director. The "God's Acre" around it held many a noted man and woman. Yet, as it is so far from the ground in which we are now concerning ourselves, it seems a bit out of place perhaps. But one must perforce show the English church's beginnings, soon to find a more solid basis in St. John's Chapel, dear to all New Yorkers even nowadays when we behold it menaced by that unholy juggernaut, the subway.

St. John's was begun in 1803 and completed in 1807. It was Part of the old King's Farm, originally granted to Trinity by Queen Anne, who appears to have done quite a lot for New York, take it all in all. It was modelled after St. Martin's-in-the-Fields, in London, and always stood for English traditions and ideals. This did not prevent the British from capturing the organ designed for it and holding it up for ransom in the War of 1812. The organ was made in Philadelphia, but was captured en route by the British ship *Plantagenet*, a cruiser with seventy-four guns, which was in the habit of picking up little boats and holding them at $100 to $200 each. Luckily the church bell had been obtained before the war!

In regard to the organ, the *Weekly Register* of Baltimore has this to say:

> "A great business this for a ship of the line.... Now a gentleman might suppose that this article would have passed harmless."

St. John's Park, now obliterated and given over to the modernism of the Hudson River Railroad Company, used, in the early fifties, to be still fashionable. Old New Yorkers given to remembrance speak regretfully of the quiet and peace and beauty of the Old Park - which is no more. But St. John's is still with us, "sombre and unalterable," as one writer describes it, "a stately link between the present and the past."

And doubtless nearly everyone who reads these pages knows of St. John's famous "Dole" - the Leake Dole, which has been such a fruitful topic for newspaper writers for decades back.

John Leake and John Watts, in the year 1792, founded the Leake and Watts' Orphan House and John Leake, in so doing, added this curious bequest:

> "I hereby give and bequeathe unto the rector and inhabitants of the Protestant Episcopal Church of the State of New York one thousand pounds, put out at interest, to be laid out in the annual income in sixpenny wheaten loaves of bread and distributed on every Sabbath morning after divine service, to such poor as shall appear most deserving."

This charity has endured through the years and is now the trust of St. John's. I have been told - though I do not vouch for it - that the bread is given out not after divine service but very early in the morning, when the grey and silver light of the new day will not too mercilessly oppress the needy and unfortunate, some of them once very rich, who come for the Dole.

In 1822 St. Luke's was built - also a part of the elastic Trinity Parish, and probably the best-known church, next to old St. John's, that stands in Greenwich Village today.

The prejudices of the English Church in early New York prevented the Catholics from gaining any sort of foothold until after the British evacuation. In 1783 St. Peter's, the first Roman Catholic Church, was erected at Barclay Street, and much trouble they had, if account may be relied on. The reported tales of an escaped nun did much to inflame the bigoted populace, but this passed, and today St. Joseph's, which was built in 1829, stands on the corner of Washington

Place and Sixth Avenue.

It is not far away, by the bye, that the old Jewish cemetery is to be found. Alderman Curran quaintly suggested that an unwarned stranger might easily stub his toe on the little graveyard on Eleventh Street. It is Beth Haim, the Hebrew Place of Rest, close to Milligan Lane. The same Eleventh Street, which (as we shall see later) was badly handicapped by "the stiff-necked Mr. Henry Brevoort" cut half of Beth Haim away. But a corner of it remains and tranquil enough it seems, not to say pleasant, though almost under the roar of the Elevated.

The Presbyterian churches got a foothold fairly early; - probably the first very fashionable one was that on Mercer Street. Its pastor, the Reverend Thomas Skinner, is chiefly, but deservedly, renowned for a memorable address he made to an assembly of children, some time in 1834. Here is an extract which is particularly bright and lucid:

> "Catechism is a compendium of divine truth. Perhaps, children, you do not know the meaning of that word. Compendium is synonymous with synopsis"!!!

The old Methodist churches were models of Puritanism. In the beginning they met in carpenter shops, or wherever they could. When they had real churches, they, for a long time, had separate entrances for the sexes.

It was after I had read of this queer little side shoot of asceticism that I began to fully appreciate what a friend of mine had said to me concerning the New Greenwich.

"The Village," he said, "is a protest against Puritanism." And, he added: "It's just an island, a little island entirely surrounded by hostile seas!"

The Village, old and new, *is* a protest. It is a voice in the wilderness. Some day perhaps it will conquer even the hostile

Anna Alice Chapin

seas. Anyway, most of the voyagers on the hostile seas will come to the Village eventually, so *it* should worry!

The Green Village is green no longer, except in scattered spots where the foliage seems to bubble up from the stone and brick as irrepressibly as Minetta Water once bubbled up thereabouts. But it is still the Village, and utterly different from the rest of the city. Not all the commissioners in the world could change the charming, erratic plan of it; not the most powerful pressure of modern business could destroy its insistent, yet elusive personality. The Village has always persistently eluded incorporation in the rest of the city. Never forget this: Greenwich was developed as independently as Boston or Chicago. It is not New York proper: it is an entirely separate place. At points, New York overflows into it, or it straggles out into New York, but it is first and foremost itself. It is not changeless at all, but its changes are eternal and superbly independent of, and inconsistent with, metropolitan evolution.

There was a formative period when, socially speaking, the growth of Greenwich was the growth of New York. But that was when Greenwich was almost the whole of fashionable New York. Later New York plunged onward and left the green cradle of its splendid beginnings. But the cradle remained, still to cherish new lives and fresh ideals and a society profoundly different, yet scarcely less exclusive in its way, than that of the Colonies. It has been described by so many writers in so many ways that one is at a loss for a choice of quotations. Perhaps the most whimsically descriptive is in O. Henry's "Last Leaf."

> "In a little district west of Washington Square the streets have run crazy and broken themselves into small strips called 'places.' These 'places' make strange angles and curves. One street crosses itself a time or two. An artist once discovered a valuable possibility in this street. Suppose a collector with a bill for paint, paper and canvas should, in traversing this route, suddenly meet himself coming back, without a cent having been paid on account!"

And Kate Jordan offers this concerning Waverly Place:

"Here Eleventh and Fourth streets, refusing to be separated by arithmetical arrangements, meet at an unexpected point as if to shake hands, and Waverly Place sticks its head in where some other street ought to be, for all the world like a village busybody who has to see what is happening around the corner."

But what of the spirit of Greenwich? The truth is that first and foremost Greenwich is the home of romance. It is a sort of Make Believe Land which has never grown up, and which will never learn to be modern and prosaic.

It is full of romance. You cannot escape it, no matter how hard you try to be practical. You start off on some commonplace stroll enough - or you tell yourself it will be so; you are in the middle of cable car lines and hustling people and shouting truck drivers, and street cleaners and motors and newsboys, and all the component parts of a modern and seemingly very sordid city - when, lo and behold, a step to the right or left has taken you into another country entirely - I had well-nigh said another world. Where did it come from - that quaint little house with the fanlight over the door and the flower-starred grassplot in front? Did it fall from the skies or was it built in a minute like the delectable little house in "Peter Pan"? Neither. It has stood there right along for half or three-quarters of a century, only you didn't happen to know it. You have stepped around the corner into Greenwich Village, that's all.

"In spots there is an unwonted silence, as though one were in some country village," says Joseph Van Dyke. "... There are scraps of this silence to be found about old houses, old walls, old trees."

Here, as in the fairy tales, all things become possible. You know that a lady in a mob-cap and panniers is playing inside that shyly curtained window. Hark! You can hear the thin, delicate notes quite plainly: this is such a quiet little street. A piano rather out of tune? Perish the thought! Dear friend, it is a spinet, - a harpsichord. Almost you can smell pot-pourri.

Perhaps it was of such a house that H.C. Bunner wrote:

> *"We lived in a cottage in old Greenwich Village,*
> *With a tiny clay plot that was burnt brown and hard;*
> *But it softened at last to my girl's patient tillage,*
> *And the roses sprang up in our little backyard;"*

The garden hunger of the Village! It is something pathetic and yet triumphant, pitiful and also splendid. It is joyous life and growth hoping in the most unpromising surroundings: it is eager and gallant hope exulting in the very teeth of defeat. Do you remember John Reed's -

> *"Below's the barren, grassless, earthen ring*
> *Where Madame, with a faith unwavering*
> *Planted a wistful garden every spring, -*
> *Forever hoped-for, - never blossoming."*

Yet they do blossom, those hidden and usually unfruitful garden-places. Sometimes they bloom in real flowers that anyone can see and touch and smell. Sometimes they come only as flowers of the heart - which, after all, will do as well as another sort, - in Greenwich Village, where they know how to make believe.

Here is how Hugh Macatamney describes Greenwich:

> "A walk through the heart of this interesting locality - the American quarter, from Fourteenth Street down to Canal, west of Sixth Avenue - will reveal a moral and physical cleanliness not found in any other semi-congested part of New York; an individuality of the positive sort transmitted from generation to generation; a picturesqueness in its old houses, 'standing squarely on their right to be individual' alongside those of modern times, and, above all else, a truly American atmosphere of the pure kind."

He adds:

> "Please remember, too, that in 1816 Greenwich Village had individualism enough to be the terminus of a stage line from Pine Street and Broadway, the stages 'running on the even hours from Greenwich and the uneven hours from Pine Street.'"

You walk on through Greenwich Village and you will expect romance to meet you. Even the distant clang of a cable car out in the city will not break the spell that is on you now. And if you have a spark of fancy, you will find your romance. You cannot walk a block in Greenwich without coming on some stony wall, suggestive alley, quaint house or vista or garden plot or tree. Everything sings to you there; even the poorest sections have a quaint glamour of their own. It gleams out at you from the most forbidding surroundings. Sometimes it is only a century-old door knocker or an ancient vine-covered wall - but it is a breath from the gracious past.

And as you cannot go a step in the Village without seeing something picturesque so you cannot read a page of the history of Greenwich without stumbling upon the trail of romance or adventure. As, for example, the tale of that same Sir. Peter Warren, whose name we have encountered more than once before, as proper a man as ever stepped through the leaves of a Colonial history and the green purlieus of Old Greenwich!

# CHAPTER III

## THE GALLANT CAREER OF SIR. PETER WARREN

"... Affection with truth must say
That, deservedly esteemed in private life,
And universally renowned for his public conduct,
The judicial and gallant Officer
Possessed all the amiable qualities of the
Friend, the Gentleman, and the Christian...."

- From the epitaph written for Sir. Peter's tomb in Westminster Abbey by Dr. Samuel Johnson.

The sea has always made a splendid romantic setting for a gallant hero. Even one of moderate attainments and inconsiderable adventures may loom to proportions that are quite picturesque when given a background of tossing waves, "all sails set," and a few jolly tars to sing and fight and heave the rope. And when you have a hero who needs no augmenting of heroism, no spectacular embellishment as it were, - what a gorgeous figure he becomes, to be sure!

Peter Warren, fighting Irish lad, venturesome sailor, sometime Admiral and Member of Parliament, and at all times a merry and courageous soldier of the high seas, falls heir to as pretty and stirring a reputation as ever set a gilded aureole about the head of a man. Though he was in the British navy and a staunch believer in "Imperial England," he was so closely associated with New York for so many years that no book about the city could be written without doing him some measure of honour. No figure is so fit as Sir. Peter's to represent those picturesque Colonial days when the "Sons of Liberty" had not begun to assemble, and this New York of ours was well-nigh as English as London town itself. So, resplendent in his gold-laced uniform and the smartly imposing hat of his rank and office, let him enter and make his bow, - Admiral Sir. Peter Warren, by your leave, Knight of the Bath, Member of Parliament, destined to lie at last in the stately gloom of the Abbey, with the rest of the illustrious English dead.

He came of a long line of Irishmen, and certainly did that fine fighting race the utmost credit. From his boyhood he was always hunting trouble; he dearly loved a fight, and gravitated into the British navy as inevitably as a duck to water. He was scarcely more than an urchin when he became a fighting sailor, and indeed one could expect no less, for both his father and grandfather had been officers in the service, and goodness knows how many lusty Warrens before them! For our friend Peter was a Warren of Warrenstown, of the County Meath just west of Dublin, and let me tell you that meant something!

The Warrens got their estates in the days of "Strongbow," and held them through all the vicissitudes of olden Ireland. They were a house called "English-Irish," and "inside the pale," which means that they stood high in British favour, and contributed heroes to the army or navy from each of their hardy generations. They had no title, but to be The Warren of Warrenstown, Meath, was to be entitled to look down with disdain upon upstart baronets and newly created peers. Sir. Christopher Aylmer's daughter, Catherine, was honoured to marry Captain Michael Warren, and her brother, Admiral Lord Aylmer, only too glad to take charge of her boy Peter later on.

Peter was the youngest of a family, composed with one exception of boys, and the most ambitious of the lot. When he was nine years old (he was born in 1703, by the bye), his father, Captain Michael, died, and three years later the oldest son, Oliver, decided to send Peter to his uncle Lord Aylmer to be trained for the service. Is it far-fetched to assume that Oliver found his small brother something of a handful? If Peter was one-quarter as pugnacious and foolhardy at twelve as he was at forty, there is small wonder that a young man burdened with the cares of a large estate and an orphaned family would be not unwilling to get rid of him, - or at least of the responsibility of him. Their uncle, the Admiral, apparently liked his little Irish nephew, and proceeded to train him for a naval career, with such vigourous success that at fourteen our young hero volunteered for His Majesty's service, - a thing, we may take it, which had been the high dream of his boyish life.

And it was real service too. Boys turned into men very quickly in those days. In Southern and African waters young Peter saw plenty of action. He had such adventures as our modern boys sit up at night to read of. For there were pirates to be encountered then, flesh-and-blood pirates with black flags and the rest of it. And deep-sea storms meant more in those days of sails and comparatively light vessels than we can even imagine today. So swiftly did Peter grow up under this stern yet thrilling education with the English colours, that after four short years he was a lieutenant. And in another six, at an age when most young men are barely standing on the threshold of their life-work, he was posted a full captain and given his first command!

His ship was H.M.S. *Grafton*, of seventy guns, - no small honour for a boy of hardly twenty-four, - and it proved to be no empty honour either. No sooner had he been posted captain than he was ordered into action. At that time there were signal and violent differences of opinion between England and other countries, - notably Spain and France. Gibraltar was the subject of one of them, it may be recalled. It was to Gibraltar that Captain Warren and his good ship *Grafton* were ordered. And when Sir. Charles Wager seized that historic bone of contention, Peter was with the fleet that did the seizing.

From that moment he was in the thick of trouble wherever it was to be found, like the dear, daredevil young Irishman that he was! Just a moment let us pause to try to visualise this youthful adventurer of ours, with the courtly manners, the irrepressible boyish recklessness and the big heart. Our only authentic descriptions of him are of a Peter Warren many years older; our only even probable likenesses are the same. But let us take these, and reckoning backward see what a man of such characteristics must have been like in his early twenties.

A delightful old print ostensibly representing him at forty, shows him to have been a round-faced, more or less portly gentleman, with a full, pleasant mouth and very big and bright eyes. His wig is meticulously curled and powdered, and he is, plainly, a very fine figure of a man indeed. Roubilliac's bust of him in Westminster makes him much better looking and not nearly, so stout. Thomas Janvier, who has written delightfully about our captain, disturbs me by insisting that he was a little man, - nay, his insult goes deeper: he says a little, *fat* man! I simply will not accept such a distressing theory!

Edward de Lancey, descended from the family of the girl Peter married, describes him as being "... Of attractive manners, quick in perception and action, but clear-headed and calm in judgment." And the historian Parkman declares that at forty-two he had "the ardour of youth still burning within him." Reverse the figures. What do you suppose that ardour was like when he was not forty-two but twenty-four?

At the time of our hero's first command and first naval engagement on his own ship, things were quite exciting for his King and country, though we have most of us forgotten that such excitements ever existed. England had a host of enemies, some of them of her own household. It was even whispered that the American possessions were not entirely and whole-heartedly loyal! This seemed incredible, to be sure, but the men in high places kept an eye on them just the same. Captain

Anna Alice Chapin

Warren's first official post was the station of New York, and in 1728 he made his first appearance in this harbour.

He was then just twenty-five, and gloriously adventurous. One can imagine with what a thrill he set sail for a new country, new friends, new excitements! I wonder if he guessed that the lady of his heart awaited him in that unknown land, as well as the dear home where, for all his sea-roving taste, he was to return again and again through twenty rich years? He was in command of the frigate *Solebay* then, and in the old papers we read many mentions of both ship and officer. From almost the first Peter loved the Colonies and the Colonies loved him. In between his cruises and battles he kept coming back like a homing bird, and every time he came he seemed to have won a little more glory with his various ships, - the sloop *Squirrel*, the frigate *Launceston*, and the big ship *Superbe* with sixty guns. It is said that no man save only the Governor himself made so fine an appearance as young Captain Warren, and fair ladies vied with each other for his attentions! Nevertheless, his social successes at this time were nothing to what was to come, when he had more money to spend!

Two years after his first introduction to New York, the Common Council of the city voted to him "the freedom of the city," from which one gathers some idea of his standing in public favour! And in another year, - of course, - he got married, and to one of the prettiest girls in the town, Susanna de Lancey!

Janvier says that the marriage did not take place until 1744, but other authorities place it at thirteen years earlier. It is much more probable that Peter got married at twenty-eight than at forty-one; I scarcely think that he could have escaped so long!

Susanna's father was Monsieur Etienne de Lancey, a Huguenot refugee, who had fled from Catholic France to the more liberal Colonies, and settled here. He soon changed the Etienne to Stephen, married the daughter of one of the old Dutch houses (Van Cortlandt) and went into business. Just what his occupation was is not clear, but later he acted as agent for Captain Warren in the disposal of his war prizes. His sons, James and Oliver, were intimate friends of Peter's through life, and, as will be seen, they worked together most zestfully when in later years the captain's boundless energies took a turn at politics.

So gallant Irish-English Peter and lovely French-Dutch Susanna were married and, we believe, lived happily ever after. They lived in New York town proper, but I conceive that, like other young lovers, they made many a trip out into the country, and that it was their dream to live there one day when they should be rich. Certain it is that as soon as our hero did get a little money at last he could hardly wait to buy the farm land far out of town on the river. But that time was not yet.

Needless to say, Peter's married life, happy as it was, could not keep him long on shore. We keep finding his name and the names of his ships in the delicious old newspapers of his day: Captain Warren has just arrived; Captain Warren's ship has "gone upon the careen" (i.e., is being repaired); Captain Warren is sailing next week, and so on, and so on. The New York *Gazette* for May 31, 1736, states that: "On Saturday last, Captain Warren in His Majesty's ship the Squirrel arrived here in eight weeks from England." One perceives that this was record time, and worth a journalistic paragraph!

Troubles becoming more rife with Spain in 1739, Peter begged for active service and got it. This probably was the beginning of his great prosperity, though his wealth did not become sensational until nearly five years later. Fortunes were constantly being made in prize ships in those days, and you may be sure that our enterprising sea-fighter was not behind other men in this or in anything else calling for initiative and daring! At all events the records seem to show that he bought his lands in the Green Village, - Greenwich, - about 1740, when he was thirty-seven. Whether he built his house at that early date is not clear, but he probably didn't have money enough yet, for when he did build, it was on a magnificent

Anna Alice Chapin

scale. In 1744, however, came his golden harvest time!

It was a little after midwinter of that year that Sir. Chaloner Ogle made him commodore of a sixteen-ship squadron in the waters of the Leeward Islands where there was decidedly good hunting in the way of prize ships. Off Martinique were many French and Spanish boats simply waiting, it would almost seem, to be eaten alive by the enemy's cruisers; and Captain Peter who had the sound treasure-hunting instinct of your born adventurer, proceeded to gobble them up! In the four months that rolled jovially by between the middle of February and the middle of June, the Captain captured twenty-four of these prizes, one alone with a plate cargo valued at two hundred and fifty thousand pounds! Ah, but those were the rare days for a stout-hearted seafaring man, with a fleet of strong boats and an expensive taste!

Captain Warren brought his prizes to New York and handed them over to his father-in-law's firm, - advertised in the old papers as "Messieurs Stephen de Lancey and Company," - who acted as his agents in practically all of what Janvier disrespectfully styles "his French and Spanish swag"! Governor Clinton had exempted prizes from duty, so it was all clear profit. With the proceeds of the excellent deals which De Lancey made for him, he then proceeded to cut the swathe for which he was by temperament and attributes so well fitted.

There never was an Irishman yet, nor a sailor either, who could not spend money in the grand manner. Our Captain was no exception, be certain! He figures superbly in the social accounts of the day; it is safe to assert that he set the pace after a fashion, and fair Mistress Susanna was a real leader of real Colonial dames! He appears to have been a genuinely and deservedly popular fellow, our Peter Warren, throwing his prize money about with a handsome lavishness, and upholding the honour of the British navy as gallantly in American society as ever he had in hostile waters abroad.

And now for that dream of a country home! Warren had lands

on the Mohawk River and elsewhere, but his heart had always yearned for the tract of land in sylvan Greenwich. In that quiet little hamlet on the green banks of the Hudson the birds sang and the leaves rustled, and the blue water rested tired eyes. Peter at this time owned nearly three hundred acres of ground there and now that he had money in plenty, he lost no time in building a glorious dovecote for himself and Mistress Susanna - a splendid house in full keeping with his usual large way of doing things.

Stroll around the block that is squared by the present Charles, Perry, Bleecker and Tenth streets some day, look at the brick and stone, the shops and boarding-houses, - and try to dream yourself back into the eighteenth century, when, in that very square of land, stood the Captain's lovely country seat. In those days it was something enormous, palatial, and indeed was always known as the Mansion or Manse. This is, of course, the basis for the silly theory that Greenwich got its name from the estate. Undoubtedly the Warren place was the largest and most important one out there, and for a time to "go out to visit at Greenwich," meant to go out to visit the Manse. For years the Captain and the Captain's lady lived in this beautiful and restful place with three little daughters to share their money, their affections and their amiable lives. Thomas Janvier's description of the house as he visualises it with his rich imagination is too charming not to quote in part:

"The house stood about three hundred yards back from the river, on ground which fell away in a gentle slope towards the waterside. The main entrance was from the east; and at the rear - on the level of the drawing-room and a dozen feet or so above the sloping hillside - was a broad veranda commanding the view westward to the Jersey Highlands and southward down the bay to the Staten Island Hills." The fanciful description goes on to picture Captain Warren sitting on this veranda, "smoking a comforting pipe after his mid-day dinner; and taking with it, perhaps, as seafaring gentlemen very often did in those days, a glass or two of substantial rum-and-water to keep everything below hatches well stowed. With what approving eye must he have regarded the trimly kept lawns and gardens below him; and with what eyes of affection the *Launceston*, all a-taunto, lying out in the stream!"

I have called the description of the house "fanciful," but it is really not that, since the old house fell into Abraham Van Nest's hands at a later date, and stood there for over a century, with the poplars, for which it was famous, and the box hedges, in which Susanna had taken such pride, growing more beautiful through the years. Not until 1865 was the lovely place destroyed by the tidal wave of modern building.

The Captain kept his town house as well, - the old Jay place, on the lower end of Broadway, but it was at the Manse that he loved best to stay, and the Manse which was and always remained his real and beloved home. In 1744 his seaman's restlessness again won over his domestic tranquillity and he was off once more in search of fresh adventures and dangers. Says the *Weekly Post Boy*, of August 27th, in that year:

"His Majesty's ship *Launceston*, commanded by the brave Commodore Warren (whose absence old Oceanus seems to lament), being now sufficiently repaired, will sail in a few days in order once more to pay some of His Majesty's enemies a visit."

And it winds up with this burst:

*"The sails are spread; see the bold warrior comes
To chase the French and interloping Dons!"*

It was in the following year that he signally distinguished himself in the historic Siege of Louisbourg, winning himself a promotion to the rank of Rear Admiral of the Blue, and a knighthood as well! It may seem a far cry from Greenwich, New York, to Louisbourg, but we cannot pass over the incident without sparing it a little space. Let me beg your patience, - quoting, in my own justification, no less a historian than James Grant Wilson:

> "This Commodore Warren was one of those indefatigable and nervous spirits who did such wonders at Louisbourg, and it is with particular pride that his achievement should be remembered in a history of New-York, as he was the only prominent New-Yorker that contributed to Massachusetts' greatest Colonial achievement."

The capture of Louisbourg may be remembered by some history readers as a part of that English-French quarrel of 1745, commonly known as "King George's War," and also as the undertaking described by so many contemporaries as "Shirley's Mad Scheme." The scheme *was* rather mad; hence its appeal to Peter Warren, who was exceedingly keen about it from the beginning.

Louisbourg was a strong French fortress on Cape Breton Island, commanding the gulf of the St. Lawrence. Its value as a military stronghold was great, and besides it had long been a fine base for privateers, and was a very present source of peril to the New England fishermen off the Banks. As far back as 1741 Governor Clarke of New York had urged the taking of this redoubtable French station, but it fell to the masterful Shirley, Governor of Massachusetts, finally to organise the expedition. He had Colonial militia to the tune of four thousand men, and he had Colonial boats, - nearly a hundred of them, - and he had the approval of the Crown (conveyed through the Duke of Newcastle); but he wanted leaders. For his land force he chose General Pepperrill, an eminently safe and sane type of soldier; for the sea he, with a real brain throb, thought of Captain Peter Warren. Francis Parkman says: "Warren, who had married an American woman and who owned large tracts of land on the Mohawk, was known to be a warm friend to the provinces." He was at Antigua when he received the Governor's request that he take command of the "Mad Scheme." Needless to say, the Captain was charmed with the idea, but he had no orders from the King! He refused almost weeping, and for two days was plunged in gloom. Imagine such a glorious chance for a fight going begging!

Then arrived a belated letter from Newcastle in England, telling him to "concert measures with Shirley for the annoyance of the enemy." Warren was so afraid that some future orders would be less vague, and give him less freedom, that he set sail for Boston with a haste that was feverish. He had with him three ships, - the *Mermaid* and *Launceston* of forty guns each, and the *Superbe* of sixty. But those two wretched days of delay! He fell in with a schooner from which he learned that Shirley's expedition had started without him!

I daresay, being a sailor and Irish, our Captain expressed himself exhaustively just then; but he recovered speedily and told the schooner to send him every British ship she met in her voyage; then he changed his course and beat straight for Canseau, determined to be in that expedition after all. He certainly was in it, and a brisk time he had of it, too.

At Canseau they were all tied up three weeks, drilling and waiting for the ice to break, but they were thankful to get there at all. The storms were severe, as may be gathered by this account of their efforts to get into Canseau, written by one of the men: "A very Fierce Storm of Snow, som Rain and very Dangerous weather to be so nigh ye Shore as we was; but we escaped the Rocks and that was all."

Pepperrill was thankful enough to see the Captain and his squadron, - it was four ships now, as the schooner had picked up another frigate for him, - but the two commanders were destined to rub each other very much the wrong way before they were through. Pepperrill was a man who took risks only very solemnly and with deliberation, and who was blessed with endless patience. Warren took risks with as much zest as he took rare food and rich wine, and in his swift, full and exciting life there had never been place or time for patience! When the siege actually commenced, the poor Captain nearly went wild with the inaction. He wanted to attack, to move, to do something. Pepperrill's calm judgment and slow tactics drove him distracted, and they were forever at odds in spite of a secret respect for each other. In speaking of the contrast between them, Parkman, after describing Pepperrill's careful management of the military end, says: "Warren was no less earnest than he for the success of the enterprise.... But in habits and character the two men differed widely. Warren was in the prime of life, and the ardour of youth still burned within him. He was impatient at the slow movement of the siege."

The Siege of Louisbourg started by Warren's and Pepperrill's demand that the fortress surrender, and the historic answer of Duchambon, the French commander, that they should have their answer from the cannon's mouth. It is not my purpose to tell of it in detail, for it lasted forty-seven days and strained the nerves of everyone to the breaking point. But one or two things happened in the time which, to my mind, make our Captain seem a very human person. There was, for instance, his amazing kindness, as unfailing to his captives as to his own men. When the great French man-of-war *Vigilant* came to the aid of the beleaguered fortress, Warren joyously captured the monster, in full sight of Louisbourg and under the big guns there. It was this incident, by the bye, for which he was knighted afterwards. The French captain, Marquis de la Maisonfort, who was Warren's prisoner, wrote in a letter to Duchambon: "The Captain and officers of this squadron treat us, not as their prisoners, but as their good friends."

Warren went wild with rage when he heard of the horrors that had befallen an English scouting party which had fallen into the hands of a band of Indians and Frenchmen, and hideously tortured. He wrote stern protests to Duchambon, and it was at this time that he urged Pepperrill most earnestly to attack. But the more phlegmatic officer could not see it in that way. Warren then argued with increasing heat that by this time the French reinforcements must be near, and could easily steal up under cover of the fog which was thick there every night. When Pepperrill still objected he lost his temper entirely, and said and wrote a number of peppery things. "I am sorry," he said, "that no one plan, though approved by all my captains, has been so fortunate as to meet your approbation or have any weight with you!"

Pepperrill explained imperturbably that Warren was trying to take too much authority upon himself. Captain Peter sent him a furious note: "I am sorry to find a kind of jealousy which I thought you would never conceive of me. And give me leave to tell you I don't want at this time to acquire reputation, as I flatter myself mine has been pretty well established long before!"

And then, as full of temper as a hot-headed schoolboy, he brought out a letter from Governor Shirley expressing regret that Captain Warren could not take command of the whole affair, - "which I doubt not would be a most happy event for His Majesty's service."

Even this could not shake the General's superhuman calm. He was indeed so quiet about it, and so uniformly polite, that his fiery associate was simply obliged to cool off. He was of too genuinely fine fibre to bear a grudge or to make a hard situation harder, and he consented to compromise, saying truly that at such times it was "necessary not to Stickle at Trifles!"

At last the time came for action, and on the seventeenth of June they took Louisbourg, in a most brilliant and stirring manner, and Warren was so wild with delight that he could not contain himself. He scribbled a note to Pepperrill which sounds like the note of a rattle-pated college lad instead of a distinguished naval commander: "We will soon keep a good house together, and give the Ladys of Louisbourg a gallant Ball."

He probably gave that ball, too, though there doesn't seem to be any record of it. He certainly had a beautiful time going about making speeches to the troops, amid much cheering; and dispensing casks of rum in which to drink his health and King George's! He was made the English Governor of the fortress temporarily, and when the news of their capture reached England both commanders were knighted and Peter Warren was made Rear Admiral of the Blue.

And in the height of the excitement a ship arrived at Louisbourg one fine day bearing Susanna herself, who had come in person to see that the hero of the day was really safe and sound!

A letter written from Louisbourg on September 25th, and published in the *Weekly Post Boy*, gives this account:

> "... The King has made the General a baronet of Great Britain; and 'tis said Mr. Warren will be one also, who is recommended by the Lords Justices to the King of Governor of this Place, and is made Rear Admiral of the Blue: He hoisted his Flag yesterday Afternoon on the Superbe, when he was saluted by the Ships in the Harbour, and the Grand Battery."

Soon after, - if we may trust James Grant Wilson's history, - he did indeed receive the Order of the Bath, and so henceforward we must give him his title, - Admiral Sir. Peter Warren, no less! After he came home from Louisbourg, the city of New York was so well pleased with him that the council voted him some extra land, - which he really did not need in the least, having plenty already.

At least one more exploit was to be added to the wreath of Peter Warren's brave enterprises in behalf of his King and country. In 1747 the French again became troublesome. A fleet of French men-of-war under one La Jonquiere, an able commander, was ordered to go and retake Louisbourg, - that, at least, among other things. Sir. Peter went to join the English commander, Anson, off Cape Finisterre, - (the "End of the Earth") and acquitted himself there so gallantly and effectively that again his country rang with praise of him, - his country which then lay on two sides of the sea. America's pride in him is shown by some of the comments in the New York press, after he had so brilliantly helped in the capture of La Jonquiere's ships. Here is, for instance, one letter from an eyewitness which was printed in the New York *Gazette*, August 31, 1747:

"I have the Honour to send you some Particulars concerning the late Engagement on 3rd Instant off Cape Finisterre; which, tho' in the greatest degree conducive to the Success of that glorious Day, yet have not been once mentioned in the publick Papers.... You may be surpriz'd, Sir, when I assert, that out of the formidable English Squadron, but seven Ships were engag'd properly speaking. Concerning the Gallantry of three of them, which were the Headmost Ships, you have already had publick accounts; and my intention by this, is to warm your hearts with an Account of the Behaviour of two others, the Devonshire, Admiral Warren's Ship, and the Bristol, commanded by Capt. Montague."

The letter goes on to describe the battle minutely, telling how Warren came boldly up to the French Commodore's ship, and attacked her, "- And, having receiv'd her fire, as terrible a one as ever I saw, ran up within Pistol-shot and then returned it, and continued a brisk fire till the enemy struck." Then, he continues, Warren "made up to the Invincible" and attacked her, later seconded by Montague. Anson, the commanding Admiral, he adds rather drily, was at least a mile astern.

In the same edition of the paper which prints this letter, we find a little side light on the way in which Lady Warren spent her days when her magnificent husband was away at the wars. Between an advertisement of "Window Crown-Glass just over from England," and "A Likely Strong Negro Wench, fit for either Town or Country Business, to be sold," we find a crisp little paragraph:

"All Persons that have any Demands on the Honourable Sir. Peter Warren, are desired to carry their accounts to his Lady, to be adjusted, and receive Payment."

Sir. Peter was, as we have seen, not a person who could sit still and peacefully do nothing. Inactivity was always a horror to him; even his domestic happiness and his wholesome joy in his wife and daughters could not entirely fill his life when he was not at sea. His first naive and childish pleasure in his immense fortune was an old story, and the King couldn't provide a battle for him every moment. The real events of his life were war cruises, but in between he began to take a hand in the politics of New York. He was high in favour with the English Throne - with some reason, we must admit - and he didn't mind stating the fact with the candour and doubtless the pride of a child of nature, as well as - who knows? - a touch of arrogance, as became a man of the world, and an English one to boot!

His brother-in-law, James de Lancey, was Chief Justice, and at sword's point with Clinton, the Governor of New York. De Lancey boasted politely but openly that he and Sir. Peter had twice as much influence in England as had Clinton, which was probably quite true. Clinton was desperately afraid of them both. Just when Clinton felt he was making a little headway Warren was called to London to enter Parliament as the member for Westminster. This gave him more prestige than ever, and the Governor moved heaven and earth to discredit him in the eyes of the Lords of Trade in London. But just then heaven and earth were personified by the British Crown and Court, and they turned deaf ears to Clinton and listened kindly to the naval hero who had made himself so prime a favourite. Clinton firmly expected and fervently feared that Warren's influence would mean his eventful overthrow and not until our hero's death did he ever draw a breath that was free from dread.

After the Revolution some of the De Lanceys lost their lands because of their loyalty to the Crown, but in Sir. Peter's time the sun shone for those who stood by the King.

But the day came speedily when Sir. Peter sailed away to return no more, and I am sure every tree in Greenwich and every cobblestone in New York mourned him!

It was in 1747 that our hero was summoned to London, to enter Parliament and from that time on was a bright particular star in English society. Known as "the richest man in England," he was a truly magnificent figure in a magnificent day. Lady Warren, who was still a beauty and a wit, was a great favourite at Court, and writers of the day declared her to be the cleverest woman in all England. Think of what golden fortunes fell to the three Warren girls, who were now of marriageable age!

They made our old friend Peter Admiral of the Red Squadron as well as an M.P., and Lady Warren so splendidly brought out her daughters that Charlotte married Willoughby, Earl of Abingdon, and Ann wed Charles Fitzroy, Baron Southampton. The youngest girl, Susanna, chose a colonel named Skinner, - and New York, still affectionately inclined toward the Admiral's daughters, named streets after the husbands of all three! Our present Christopher Street used to be Skinner Road; Fitzroy Road ran northward, near our Eighth Avenue from Fourteenth Street far uptown; Abingdon Road, which was known colloquially and prettily as "Love Lane," was far, far out in the country until much later, somewhere near Twenty-first Street. Abingdon Square alone preserves one of the old family names, and in Abingdon Square I am certain some of those dear ghosts come to walk.

And still I find that I have not told the half of Sir. Peter's story! I have not told of his adventures in the Mohawk country, where he travelled from sheer love of adventure and danger in the first place, and afterward established a fine settlement and plantation; of his placing there his sister's young son, William Johnson, later to be a great authority on matters pertaining to the Indians, and how he sent him out vast consignments of "rum and axes," to open negotiations with the Mohawks; how in his letter to his nephew he sounded a note of true Irish blarney, in cautioning him not to find fault with the horses supplied by a certain man, "since he is a relation of my wife's!"

I have not told of his narrow escape from the Indians on one dramatic occasion; nor of his trip to the West Indies as an envoy of peace; nor of his services in Barbadoes which caused the people thereof to present him with a gorgeous silver monteith, or punch-bowl; nor of the mighty dinner party he gave at which the Rev. Mr. Moody said the historic grace: "Good Lord, we have so much to be thankful for that time would be infinitely too short to do it in. We must, therefore, leave it for eternity. Amen." I have said nothing of Sir. Peter's attack of small-pox, which left his good-looking face badly marked, if we can believe the likeness modelled by Roubilliac; nor - but it would take volumes to tell the full and eventful story of this brave and gallant-hearted man, who died when he was only forty-eight, in the year 1752. It seems incredible that so much could have been crowded into so short a life. In death he was honoured quite as he deserved, for his tomb in the Abbey is a gorgeous and impressive one, and such men as the great French sculptor, and Dr. Johnson himself, had a hand in making it memorable in proportion to his greatness.

In looking over our hero's career we are struck by the absence of shadows. One would say that so unrelieved a record of success, of honour, glory, love and wealth, so much pure sunshine, so complete a lack of all trouble or defeat, must make a picture flat and characterless, insipid in its light, bright colours, insignificant in its deeper values. But it is not so. Peter Warren, the spoiled child of fortune, was something more than a child of fortune, since he won his good things of life always at the risk of that life which he enriched; and surely, no obstinately fortuitous twist of circumstances could ever really spoil him.

His honestly heroic qualities are his passport. He cannot seem smug, nor colourless, nor over-prosperous: he is too vivid and too vigorous. His childish vanity is nobly discounted by his childlike simplicity in facing big issues. The blue and gold which he wore so magnificently can never to us be the mere trappings of rank: they carry on them the shadows of battle smoke, and the rust of enviable wounds. Let us take his memory then gladly, and with true homage, rejoicing that its record of happiness appears as stainless as its history of honour, and well satisfied to find one picture in which something of the sunshine of high gallantry seems caught, and for all time.

Dr. Johnson wrote thirty lines of eulogy of him, with the nicety and distinction of phrase which one would expect. Perhaps the simple ending of it is most impressive of all; so let us make it our own for the occasion:

> *"... But the ALMIGHTY,*
> *Whom alone he feared, and whose gracious protection*
> *He had often experienced,*
> *Was pleased to remove him from a place of Honour,*
> *To an eternity of happiness,*
> *On the 29th day of July, 1752,*
> *In the 49th year of his age."*

# CHAPTER IV

## THE STORY OF RICHMOND HILL

If my days of fancy and romance were not past, I could find here an ample field for indulgence!

- ABIGAIL ADAMS, writing from Richmond Hill House, in 1783.


I had left dear St. John's, - for this time my pilgrim feet were turned a bit northward to a shrine of romance rather than religion. I meandered along Canal, and traversed Congress Street. Congress, by the bye, is about two yards long; do you happen to know it?

In a few moments, I was standing in a sort of trance at that particular point of Manhattan marked by the junction of Charlton and Varick streets and the end of Macdougal, about two hundred feet north of Spring. And there was nothing at all about the scenic setting, you would surely have said, to send anyone into any kind of a trance.

On one side of me was an open fruit stall; on another, a butcher's shop; the Cafe Gorizia (with windows flagrant with pink confectionery), and the two regulation and indispensable saloons to make up the four corners.

In a sentimentally reminiscent mood, I took out a notebook,

Anna Alice Chapin

to write down something of my impressions and fancies. But there was a general murmur of war-inflamed suspicion, and I desisted and fled. How was I to tell them that there, where I stood, in that very citified and very nearly squalid environment (it was raining that day too), I could yet see, quite distinctly, the shadowy outlines of the one-time glorious House of Richmond Hill?

They were high gates and ornate, one understands. I visualised them over and against the dull and dingy modern buildings. Somewhere near here where I was standing, the great drive-way had curved in between the tall fretted iron posts, to that lovely wooded mound which was the last and most southern of the big Zantberg Range, and seemingly of a rare and rich soil. The Zantberg, you remember, started rather far out in the country, - somewhere about Clinton Place and Broadway, - and ran south and west as far as Varick and Van Dam streets.

I had passed on Downing Street one house at least which looked as though it had been there forever and ever, but just here it was most commonplace and present-century in setting, and the roar of traffic was in my ears. But I am sure that I saw Richmond Hill House plainly, - that distinguished structure which was described by an eyewitness as "a wooden building of massive architecture, with a lofty portico supported by Ionic columns, the front walls decorated with pilasters of the same order and its whole appearance distinguished by a Palladian character of rich though sober ornament." We learn further that its entrance was broad and imposing, that there were balconies fronting the rooms on the second story. The inside of the house was spaciously partitioned, with large, high rooms, massive stairways with fine mahogany woodwork, and a certain restful amplitude in everything which was a feature of most of the true Colonial houses.

Thomas Janvier quotes from some anonymous writer of an earlier day: "From the crest of this small eminence was an enticing prospect; on the south, the woods and dells and winding road from the lands of Lispenard, through the valley where was Borrowson's tavern; and on the north and west the plains of Greenwich Village made up a rich prospect to gaze on."

Lispenard's Salt Meadows lie still, I suppose, under Canal Street North. I have not been able to place exactly Borrowson's tavern. Our old friend, Minetta Water, which flowed through the site of Washington Square, made a large pond at the foot of Richmond Hill, - somewhere about the present junction of Bedford and Downing streets. In winter it offered wonderful skating; in summer it was a dream of sylvan loveliness, and came to be called Burr's Pond, after that enigmatic genius who later lived in the house.

One more description - and the best - of Richmond Hill as it was the century before last; this one written by good Mistress Abigail, wife of John Adams, one-time vice-president of the United States, during their occupancy of the place. Said she, openly adoring the Hill at all times:

"In natural beauty it might vie with the most delicious spot I ever saw. It is a mile and a half from the city of New York. The house stands upon an eminence; at an agreeable distance flows the noble Hudson, bearing upon its bosom innumerable small vessels laden with the fruitful productions of the adjacent country. Upon my right hand are fields beautifully variegated with grass and grain, to a great extent, like the valley of Honiton in Devonshire. Upon my left the city opens to view, intercepted here and there by a rising ground and an ancient oak. In front beyond the Hudson, the Jersey shores present the exuberance of a rich, well-cultivated soil. In the background is a large flower-garden, enclosed with a hedge and some every handsome trees. Venerable oaks and broken ground covered with wild shrubs surround me, giving a natural beauty to the spot which is truly enchanting. A lovely variety of birds serenade me morning and evening, rejoicing in their liberty and security."

Anna Alice Chapin

The historian, Mary L. Booth, commenting on the above, says:

"This rural picture of a point near where Charlton now crosses Varick Street naturally strikes the prosaic mind familiar with the locality at the present day as a trick of the imagination. But truth is stranger, and not infrequently more interesting, than fiction."

And now go back to the beginning.

A very large section of this part of the island was held under the grant of the Colonial Government, by the Episcopal Church of the city of New York - later to be known more succinctly as Trinity Church Parish. St. John's, - not built at that time, of course - is part of the same property. This particular portion (Richmond Hill), as we may gather from the enthusiastic accounts of those who had seen it, must have been peculiarly desirable. At any rate, it appealed most strongly to one Major Abraham Mortier, at one time commissary of the English army, and a man of a good deal of personal wealth and position.

In 1760, Major Mortier acquired from the Church Corporation a big tract including the especial hill of his desires and, upon it, high above the green valleys and the silver pond, he proceeded to put a good part of his considerable fortune into building a house and laying out grounds which should be a triumph among country estates.

That he was a personage of importance goes without saying, for His Majesty's forces had right of way in those days, in all things social as well as governmental. He proceeded to entertain largely, as soon as he had his home ready for it, and so it was that at that time Richmond Hill established its deathless reputation for hospitality.

Mortier did not buy the property outright but got it on a very long lease. Though his first name sounds Hebraic and his last Gallic, he was, we may take it, a thoroughly British soul, for he called it Richmond Hill to remind him of England. The people of New York used to gossip excitedly over the small fortune he spent on those grounds, the house was the most pretentious that the neighbourhood had boasted up to that time. Of course the Warren place was much farther north, and this particular locality was only just beginning to be fashionable.

A friend of the Commissary's, and a truly illustrious visitor at the Hill, was Sir. Jeffrey Amherst, later Lord Amherst. He made Mortier's house his headquarters at the close of his campaigns waged against French power in America. He is really not so well known as he should be, for in those tangled beginnings of our country we can hardly overestimate the importance of any one determined or strategic move, and it is due to Amherst, very largely, that half of the State of New York was not made a part of Canada. Incidentally, Amherst College is named for him.

The worthy Commissary died, it is believed, at about the time that trouble started. On April 13th, in the memorable year 1776, General Washington made "the Hill" his headquarters, and the house built by the British army official was the scene of some of the most stirring conferences that marked the beginning of the Revolution.

At the vitally important officers' councils held behind those tall, white columns, there was one man so unusual, so brilliant, so incomprehensible, that a certain baffling interest if not actual romance attaches itself automatically to the bare utterance or inscription of his name, - Aaron Burr. He was aide-de-camp to General Putnam, and already had a vivid record behind him. It was during Washington's occupancy of Richmond Hill that Burr grew to love the place which was later to be his own home.

I confess to a very definite weakness for Aaron Burr. Few hopeless romanticists escape it. Dramatically speaking, he is one of the most striking figures in American history, and I imagine that I have not been the first dreamer of dreams and writer of books who has haunted the scenes of his flesh-and-blood activity in the secret, half-shamefaced hope of one day happening upon his ghost!

From the day of his graduation from college at sixteen, he somehow contrived to win the attention of everyone whom he came near. He still wins it. We love to read of his frantic rush to the colours, guardian or no guardian; of the steel in him which lifted him from a bed of fever to join the Canadian expedition; of his daring exploits of espionage disguised as a French Catholic priest; of a hundred and one similar incidents in a life history which, as we read it, is far too strange not to be true.

Spectacular he was from his birth, and even today his name upon a page is enough to set up a whole theatre in our imaginations. Just one incident comes to me at this moment. It is so closely associated with the region with which this book is concerned, that I cannot but set it down in passing.

The story runs that it was a mistake in an order which sent General Knox of Silliman's Brigade to a small fort one mile from town (that is, about Grand Street), known as "Bunker's Hill" - not to be confounded with the other and more famous "Bunker"! It happened to be a singularly unfortunate position. There was neither food nor water in proper quantities, and the munitions were almost non-existent. The enemy was on the island.

Whether Major Burr, of Putnam's division, was sent under some regular authority, or whether he characteristically had taken the matter into his own hands, the histories I have read do not tell. But they do tell of his galloping up, breathless on a lathered horse, making the little force understand the danger of their position, pleading with his inimitable eloquence and advancing the reasons for their retreat at once. The men were stubborn; they did not want to retreat. But he talked. He proved that the English could take the scrap of a fort in four hours; he exhorted and urged, and at last he won. They said they would follow him. From that moment he took charge, and led them along the Greenwich Road through the woods, skirting the swamps, fording the rivers, to Harlem, to safety and to eventual victory.

This was only one of many instances in which his wit, his eloquence, his good sense, his leadership and his unquestioned personal daring served his country and served her well.

When Washington moved his headquarters to the Roger Morris house near the Point of Rocks, a period of comparative mystery descended for a time upon Richmond Hill. During the ensuing struggle, and before the formal evacuation of New York, the house is supposed to have been occupied off and on by British officers. But in 1783 they departed for good! and in 1789, Vice-president John Adams and Mistress Abigail came to live there.

We have already read two examples of Mrs. Adams' enthusiastic outpourings in regard to Richmond Hill. She was, in fact, never tired of writing of it. A favourite quotation of hers she always applied to the place:

> *"In this path,*
> *How long soe'er the wanderer roves, each step*
> *Shall wake fresh beauties; each last point present*
> *A different picture, new, and each the same."*

That entire neighbourhood was rich in game, - we have already seen that the Dutch farmers thought highly of the duck shooting near the Sand Hill Road, and that Minetta Brook was a first-class fishing stream. Birds of all sorts were plentiful, and the Adamses did their best to preserve them on their own place. But too keen sportsmen were always stealing into the Richmond Hill grounds for a shot or two. "Oh, for game laws!" was her constant wail. In one letter she declares: "The partridge, the woodcock and the pigeon are too great temptations for the sportsman to withstand!"

And please don't forget for one moment that this was at Charlton and Varick streets!

The House on the Hill was the home of quite ceremonious entertaining in those days. John Adams, in another land, would surely have been a courtier - a Cavalier rather than a Roundhead. John T. Morse, Jr., says that the Vice-president liked "the trappings of authority." The same historian declares that in his advice to President Washington, "... he talked of dress and undress, of attendants, gentlemen-in-waiting, chamberlains, etc., as if he were arranging the household of a European monarch."

Gulian C. Verplanck (sometimes known by the nom de plume of "Francis Herbert"), wrote in 1829, quite an interesting account of Richmond Hill as he personally recalled it. He draws for us a graphic picture of a dinner party given by the Vice-president and Mrs. Adams for various illustrious guests.

After entering the house by a side door on the right, they mounted a broad staircase with a heavy mahogany railing. Dinner was served in a large room on the second floor with Venetian windows and a door opening out onto the balcony under the portico. And then he gives us these vivid little vignettes of those who sat at the great table:

In the centre sat "Vice-president Adams in full dress, with his bag and *solitaire*, his hair frizzed out each side of his face as you see it in Stuart's older pictures of him. On his right sat Baron Steuben, our royalist republican disciplinarian general. On his left was Mr. Jefferson, who had just returned from France, conspicuous in his red waistcoat and breeches, the fashion of Versailles. Opposite sat Mrs. Adams, with her cheerful, intelligent face. She was placed between the Count du Moustier, the French Ambassador, in his red-healed shoes and earrings, and the grave, polite, and formally bowing Mr. Van Birket, the learned and able envoy of Holland. There, too, was Chancellor Livingston, then still in the prime of life, so deaf as to make conversation with him difficult, yet so overflowing with wit, eloquence and information that while listening to him the difficulty was forgotten. The rest were members of Congress, and of our Legislature, some of them no inconsiderable men. Being able to talk French, a rare accomplishment in America at that time, a place was assigned to me next the count."

Verplanck goes on to describe the dinner. He says that it was a very grand affair, bountiful and elaborately served, but the French Ambassador would taste nothing. He took a spoonful or two of soup but refused everything else "from the roast beef down to the lobsters." Everyone was concerned, for that was a day of trenchermen, and only serious illness kept people from eating their dinners. At last the door opened and his own private *chef,* - quaintly described by Verplanck as "his body-cook," - rushed into the room pushing the waiters right and left before him, and placed triumphantly upon the table an immense pie of game and truffles, still hot from the oven. This obviously had been planned as a pleasant surprise for the hosts. Du Moustier took a small helping himself and divided the rest among the others. The chronicler adds, "I can attest to the truth of the story and the excellence of the *pate!*"

No one doubts the courteous intentions of the Count, but something tells me that that excellent housewife and incomparable hostess, Mistress Adams, was not enchanted by the unexpected addition to her delicious and carefully planned menu!

It is Verplanck, by the bye, who has put in a peculiarly succinct way one of the most signal characteristics of New York - its lightning-like evolution.

"In this city especially," he says, "the progress of a few years effect what in Europe is the work of centuries." A shrewd and happily tongued observer, is Mr. Verplanck; we shall have occasion, I believe, to refer to him again.

The Adams' occupancy of Richmond Hill House was, we must

Anna Alice Chapin

be convinced, a very happy one. It was a house of a flexible and versatile personality, a beautiful home, an important headquarters of many state affairs, a brilliant social nucleus. Washington and his wife often went there to call in their beloved post-chaise, and there was certainly no dignitary of the time and the place who was not at one time or another a guest there. In the course of time, the Adamses went to a new and fine dwelling at Bush Hill on the Schuylkill. And dear Mistress Abigail, faithful to the house of her heart, wrote wistfully of her just-acquired home:

> It is a beautiful place, but the grand and sublime I left at Richmond Hill" ...

In 1797, the house went to a rich foreigner named Temple. I quote the chronicles of old New York, but can give you little information concerning this gentleman. The only thing at all memorable or interesting about him seems to have been the fact that he was robbed of a large quantity of money and valuables while at the Hill, that the thieves were never discovered and that for this reason at least he filled the local press for quite a time. His occupancy seems to have been short, and, save for the robbery, uneventful (if he really was a picturesque and adventurous soul, I humbly ask pardon of his ghost, but this is all I can find out about him!) - for it was in that self-same year that the Burrs came to live at Richmond Hill, and Temple passed into obscurity as far as New York history is concerned.

Mrs. Burr, that older Theodosia who was the idol of Aaron Burr's life, had died three years before, and little Theo was now the head of his household. Have you ever read the letters that passed between these three, by the bye? They are so quaint, so human, so tender - I believe that you will agree with me that such reading has more of charm in it than the most dramatic modern novel. They bemoan their aches and pains and cheer each other up as though they were all little Theo's age. "Passed a most tedious night," writes Mrs. Burr, and adds that she has bought a pound of green tea for two dollars! And -

"Ten thousand loves. *Toujours la votre* Theodosia."

Burr writes that he has felt indisposed, but is better, thanks to a draught "composed of laudanum, nitre and other savoury drugs." When their letters do not arrive promptly they are in despair. "Stage after stage without a line!" complains Theodosia the mother, in one feverishly incoherent note. And Theodosia the daughter, even at nine years old, had her part in this correspondence.

Her father writes her that from the writing on her last envelope, he thought the letter must come from some "great fat fellow"! He advises her to write a little smaller, and says he loves to hear from her. Then he whimsically reproaches her for not saying a word about his last letter to her, nor answering a single one of his questions: "That is not kind - it is scarcely civil!"

When little Theodosia was eleven her mother died, and henceforward she was her father's housekeeper and dearest companion. She is said to have been beautiful, brilliant and fascinating even from her babyhood, and certainly the way in which she took charge of Richmond Hill at the age of fourteen would have done credit to a woman with at least another decade to her credit.

Burr had a beautiful city house besides the one on the Hill, but he and Theo both preferred the country place, and they entertained there as lavishly as the Adamses before them. Burr had a special affection for the French, and his house was always hospitably open to the expatriated aristocrats during the French Revolution. Volney stopped with him, and Talleyrand, and Louis Philippe himself. Among the Americans his most constant guests were Dr. Hosack, the Clintons, and, oddly enough, Alexander Hamilton! Hamilton, one imagines, found Burr personally interesting, though he had small use for his politics, and warned people against him as being that dangerous combination: a daring and adventurous spirit, quite without conservative principles or scruples.

Burr is described by one biographer as being "a well-dressed man, polite and confident, with hair powdered and tied in a queue." He stooped slightly, and did not move with the grace or ease one would have expected from so experienced a soldier, but he had "great authority of manner," and was uniformly "courtly, witty and charming." During one of those legal battles in which he had only one rival (Hamilton) it was reported of him that "Burr conducted the trial with the dignity and impartiality of an angel but with the rigour of a devil!"

Gen. Prosper M. Wetmore, who adores his memory and can find extenuation for anything and everything he did, writes this charming tribute:

> "Born, as it seemed, to adorn society; rich in knowledge; brilliant and instructive in conversation; gifted with a charm of manner that was almost irresistible; he was the idol of all who came within the magic sphere of his friendship and his social influence."

His enthusiastic historians fail to add that, though he does not seem to have been at all handsome, he was always profoundly fascinating to women. It is doubtful (in spite of his second marriage at seventy odd) if he ever loved anyone very deeply after his wife Theodosia's death, but it is very certain indeed that a great, great many loved him!

Richmond Hill was the scene of one exceedingly quaint incident during the very first year that Burr and his young daughter lived in it.

Burr was in Philadelphia on political business, and fourteen-year-old Theo was in charge in the great house on the Hill a mile and a half from New York. Imagine any modern father leaving his little girl behind in a more or less remote country place with a small army of servants under her and full and absolute authority over them and herself! But I take it that there are not many modern little girls like Theodosia Burr. Certainly there are very few who could translate the American

Constitution into French, and Theo did that while she was still a slip of a girl, merely to please her adored father!

Which is a digression.

In some way Burr had made the acquaintance of the celebrated Indian Chief of the Mohawks, Tha-yen-da-ne-gea. He was intelligent, educated and really a distinguished orator, and Burr took a great fancy to him. The Chief had adopted an American name, - Joseph Brant, - and had acquired quite a reputation. He was en route for Washington, but anxious to see New York before he went. So Burr sent him to Richmond Hill, and gave him a letter to present to Theo, saying that his daughter would take care of him!

The letter runs:

> "... This will be handed to you by Colonel Brant, the celebrated Indian Chief.... He is a man of education.... Receive him with respect and hospitality. He is not one of those Indians who drink rum, but is quite a gentleman; not one who will make you fine bows, but one who understands and practises what belongs to propriety and good-breeding. He has daughters - if you could think of some little present to send to one of them (a pair of earrings for example) it would please him...."

Even the prodigiously resourceful Theo was a bit taken aback by this sudden proposition. In the highly cosmopolitan circle that she was used to entertaining, she so far had encountered no savages, and, in common with most young people, she thought of "Brant" as a fierce barbarian who, - her father's letter notwithstanding, - probably carried a tomahawk and would dance a war dance in the stately hallway of Richmond Hill.

In her letter to her father, written after she had met Brant and made him welcome, she admitted that she had been paramountly worried about what she ought to give him to eat.

She declared that her mind was filled with wild ideas of (and she quotes):

> *"'The Cannibals that each other eat,*
> *The anthropophagi, and men whose heads*
> *Do grow beneath their shoulders!'"*

She had, she confesses, a vague notion that all savages ate human beings, and - though this obviously was intended as a touch of grisly humour, - had half a notion to procure a human head and have it served up in state after the mediaeval fashion of serving boars' heads in Old England!

However, she presented him with a most up-to-date and epicurean banquet, and had the wit and good taste to include in her dinner party such representative men as Bishop Moore, Dr. Bard and her father's good friend Dr. Hosack, the surgeon.

When the party was over she wrote Burr quite enthusiastically about the Indian Chief, and declared him to have been "a most Christian and civilised guest in his manners!"

There were no ladies at Theo's dinner party. She lived so much among men, and so early learned to take her place as hostess and woman that I imagine she would have had small patience with the patronage and counsel of older members of her sex. That she was extravagantly popular with men old and young is proved in many ways. Wherever she went she was a belle. Whether the male beings she met chanced to be young and stupid or old and wise, there was something for them to admire in Theo, for she was both beautiful and witty, and she had something of her father's "confidence of manner" which won adherents right and left.

Mayor Livingston took her on board a frigate in the harbour one day, and warned her to leave her usual retainers behind.

"Now, Theodosia," he admonished her with affectionate

raillery, "you must bring none of your *sparks* on board! They have a magazine there, and we should all be blown up!"

In 1801, when she was eighteen years old, the lovely Theo married Joseph Alston, an immensely rich rice planter from South Carolina, owner of more than a thousand slaves, and at one time governor of his state. Though she went to the South to live, she never could bear to sever entirely her relations with Richmond Hill. It is a curious fact that everyone who ever lived there loved it best of all the places in the world.

One year after her marriage Theo came on to New York for a visit - I suppose she stopped at her father's town house, since it was in spring, and before the country places would naturally be open. At all events it was during this visit that, fresh from her rice fields (which never agreed with her), she wrote in a letter:

"... I have just returned from a ride in the country and a visit to Richmond Hill. Never did I behold this island so beautiful. The variety of vivid greens, the finely cultivated fields and gardens, the neat, cool air of the  cit's boxes peeping through straight rows of tall poplars,  and the elegance of some gentlemen's seats, commanding a view of the majestic Hudson, and the high, dark shores of New Jersey, altogether form a scene so lovely, so touching, and to me so new, that I was in constant rapture."

In 1804 came the historic quarrel between Aaron Burr and Alexander Hamilton. Since this chapter is the story of Richmond Hill and not the life of Aaron Burr, I shall not concern myself with the whys or the wherefores of that disastrous affair.

Histories must perforce deal with the political aims, successes and failures of men; must cover a big canvas and sing a large and impersonal song. But just here we have only to think of these old-time phantoms of ours as they affect or are affected by the old-time regions in which for the nonce we are interested. To Richmond Hill - with its white columns and

Anna Alice Chapin

shadow-flinging portico, its gardens and its oak trees and its silver pond - it was of small import that the master just missed being President of the United States, that he did become Vice-president, and President of the Senate, and that he was probably as able a jurist as ever distinguished the Bar of New York; also that he made almost as many enemies as he did friends. But it was decidedly the concern of the sweet and imposing old house on Richmond Hill that it was from its arms, so to speak, that he went out in a cold, white rage to the duel with his chief enemy; that he returned, broken and heartsick, doubly defeated in that he had chanced to be the victor, to the protection of Richmond Hill.

I cannot help believing that the household gods of a man take a very special interest and a very personal part in what fortunes befall him. More than any deities of old, they live with and in him; they at once go forth with him to battle, and welcome him home. I can conceive of some hushed and gracious home-spirit walking restless by night because the heart and head of the house was afar or in danger. And a house so charged with personality as that on Richmond Hall must have had many a ghost, - of fireside and of garden close, - who wept for fallen fortunes as they had rejoiced for gaiety and bright enterprise.

Aaron Burr and Alexander Hamilton were born antagonists: their personalities, their ideals, their methods, were as diverse and as implacably divergent as the poles. Hamilton, as a statesman, believed that Burr was dangerous; and so he was: sky rockets and geniuses usually are. Hamilton did his brilliant best to destroy the other's power (it was chiefly due to his efforts that Burr missed the Presidency), and, being a notably courageous man, he was not afraid to go on warning America against him.

And so it all came about: - the exchange of letters - haughty, courteously insolent, utterly unyielding on both sides - then the challenge, and finally the duel.

I am glad to think that Theo Alston was safe among her

husband's rice fields at that time. She worshipped her father, and everything that hurt him stabbed her to her devoted heart.

It was in an early, fragrant dawn - Friday the sixth of July, 1804 - that Burr and his seconds left our beautiful Richmond Hill, where the birds were singing and the pond just waking to the morning light, for Weehawken Heights on the Jersey shore.

At about seven, Burr reached the ground which had been appointed. Just after came Hamilton with his seconds, and the surgeon, Dr. Hosack. The distance was punctiliously measured, and these directions read solemnly to the principals:

"The parties, being placed at their stations, shall present and fire when they please. If one fires before the other, the opposite second shall say 1 - 2 - 3 - fire; and he shall then fire or lose his fire."

Then came the word "Present!" from one of the witnesses. Both duellists fired and Hamilton dropped. Burr was untouched. He stood for a second looking at his fallen adversary, and then (as the story goes), "with a gesture of profound regret, left the ground...."

Back to Richmond Hill and the troubled household gods. Burr was no butcher, and he did not dislike Hamilton personally. I wonder how many times he paced the cool dining-room with the balcony outside, and how many times he refused meat or drink, before he despatched his note to Dr. Hosack? Here it is:

"Mr. Burr's respectful compliments. - He requests Dr. Hosack to inform him of the present state of General H., and of the hopes which are entertained of his recovery.

"Mr. Burr begs to know at what hour of the day the Dr. may most probably be found at home, that he may repeat his enquiries. He would take it very kind if the Dr. would take the trouble of calling on him, as he returns from

Mr. Bayard's."

On the thirteenth, the New York *Herald* published:

"With emotions that we have not a hand to inscribe, have we to announce the death of *Alexander Hamilton.*

> "He was suddenly cut off in the forty-eighth year of his age, in the full vigour of his faculties and in the midst of all his usefulness."

The inquest which followed presented many and mixed views. Samuel Lorenzo Knapp, writing in 1835, and evidently a somewhat prejudiced friend, says that "the jury of inquest at last were reluctantly dragooned into a return of murder."

Meanwhile, for eleven long black days, Burr stayed indoors at Richmond Hill. He was afraid to go out, for he knew that popular feeling was, in the main, against him. Dark times for the household gods! At last, one starless, cloudy night, having heard of the murder verdict, he stole away.

His faithful servant and friend, John Swartwout, went with him, and a small barge lay waiting for him on the Hudson just below his Richmond Hill estate, with a discreet crew. They rowed all night, and at breakfast time, he turned up at the country place of Commodore Truxton, at Perth Amboy.

Haggard and worn, he greeted his friend the Commodore with all his usual *sang-froid*, and suggested nonchalantly that he had "spent the night on the water, and a dish of coffee would not come amiss!"

He never went back to Richmond Hill to live again, though he later returned to New York and dwelt there for many years. He went, for a time, to Theo in the South, fearing arrest, but as a matter of fact, verdict or no verdict, the matter of Hamilton's death was never followed up. Burr came calmly back to the Capitol and finished his term as Vice-president. In his farewell speech to the Senate he said he did not remember the names of all the people who had slandered him and intrigued against him, since "he thanked God he had no memory for injuries!"

The year after the duel he evolved his monstrous and hare-brained plan of establishing a Southern Republic with New Orleans as Capital and himself as President. Mexico was in it too. In fact, President Jefferson himself wrote of the project: "He wanted to overthrow Congress, corrupt the navy, take the throne of Montezuma and seize New Orleans.... It is the most extraordinary since the days of Don Quixote!..."

General Wetmore loyally declares the scheme to have been "a justifiable enterprise for the conquest of one of the provinces of Southern America." But no one in the whole world really knows all about it. The sum of the matter is that he was tried for treason, and that, though he was acquitted, he was henceforward completely dead politically. Through all, Theo stood by him, and her husband too. They went to prison with him, and shared all his humiliation and disappointment. Affection? Blind, confident adoration? Never was man born who could win it more completely!

But America as a whole did not care for him any more. Dr. Hosack loaned him money, and, after his acquittal, he set sail for England, and let Richmond Hill be sold to John Jacob Astor by his creditors. It brought only $25,000, which was a small sum compared to what he owed, so he had another object in staying on the other side of the water: a quite lively chance of the Debtors' Prison!

Apropos of this, there is one rather human little tale which is comforting to read, dropped down, as it is, in the middle of so wildly brilliant a career, so colossally disastrous a destiny.

While Burr was living at Richmond Hill, he was often obliged to take coach journeys to outside points. One day he was on his way home from Albany and stopped at a roadhouse at Kingston. While he was eating and drinking and the horses were being changed, he saw a drawing which interested him. He asked to see more by the same artist, for he had a keen appreciation of skill in all lines.

This and the other sketches shown him were the work of a young fellow called John Vanderlyn, who shortly was summoned to meet the great Burr. The lad was apprenticed to a wagon-maker, and had absolutely no prospects nor any hope of cultivating his undoubted talent. Like any other boy young and poor and in a position so humble as to offer no opportunity of improvement, he was even afraid of change, and seemed unwilling to take the plunge of leaving his master and taking his chance in the great world.

"Very well," said Burr. "When you change your mind, just put a clean shirt in your pocket, come to New York and asked for Colonel Burr."

Then he dismissed the boy from his presence and the whole episode from his mind, got into his coach and continued on his way.

Two months later he was at breakfast in the dining-room at Richmond Hill, - with Theo probably pouring out his "dish of coffee," - when a vast disturbance arose downstairs. A roughly dressed lad had presented himself at the front door and insisted on seeing Colonel Burr, in spite of all the resistance of his manservant. At last he succeeded in forcing his way past, and made his appearance in the breakfast-room, followed by the startled and indignant servant. Burr did not recognise him in the least, but the youth walked up to him, pulled a shirt - of country make but quite clean - out of his coat pocket, and held it out.

Immediately it all came back to Burr, and he was delighted by the simplicity with which the wagon-maker's apprentice had taken him at his word. No one could play the benefactor more generously when he chose, and he lost no time in sending Vanderlyn to Paris to study art. So brilliantly did the young man acquit himself in the *ateliers* there that within a very few years he was the most distinguished of all American painters in Europe. In Henry Brevoort's Letters are references to his commission to paint General Jackson, among others.

And now comes the pleasant part of this little story within a story:

In 1808, Aaron Burr was an exile in London. His trouble with Hamilton, his mad scheme of empire and trial for treason, his political unpopularity, had made him an outcast; and at that time, he, the most fascinating, and at one time the most courted of men, lived and moved without a friend. And he met Vanderlyn, - once the wistful lad who drew pictures when his master wanted him to turn spokes. Now Vanderlyn was a big man, with a name in the world and money in his pocket, and - Aaron Burr's warm and grateful friend. Burr was living in lodgings at eight shillings a week at that time, and his only caller was John Vanderlyn.

In 1812 it seemed safe, even advisable, for the exile to return to America again, but where was the money to be found? He was penniless. Well, the money was found quite easily. Vanderlyn made a pile of all his best canvases, sold them, and handed over the proceeds to his friend and erstwhile benefactor. And so Burr came home to America.

I think the nicest part of all this is Vanderlyn's loyal silence about the older man's affairs. It is likely that he knew more about Burr's troubles and perplexities and mistakes than any other man, but he was fiercely reticent on the subject. Once a writer approached Vanderlyn for some special information. It was after Burr's death, and the scribe had visions of publishing something illuminating about this most mysterious and inscrutable genius.

"And now about Burr's private life," he insinuated confidentially.

Anna Alice Chapin

The artist turned on him savagely.

"You let Burr's private life alone!" he snarled.

The author fled, deciding that he certainly would do just that!

Burr came home. But fate was not through with him yet. Dear Theo set sail without delay, from South Carolina, to meet her father in New York. He had been gone years, and she was hungry for the sight of him. Her little son had died, and father and daughter longed to be together again.

Her boat was the *Patriot* - and the *Patriot* has never been heard from since she put out. She was reported sunk off Cape Hatteras, but for many years a haunting report persisted that she had been captured by the pirates that then infested coastwise trade. So Theodosia - barely thirty years old - vanished from the world so far as we may know. The dramatic and tragic mystery of her death seems oddly in keeping with her life and that of her father. Somehow one could scarcely imagine Theo growing old peacefully on a Southern plantation!

Her father never regained his old eagerness for life after her loss. He lived for years, practised law once more with distinction and success on Nassau Street, even made a second marriage very late in life, but I think some vivid, vital, romantic part of him, something of ambition and fire and adventure, was lost at sea with his child Theodosia.

And now shall we go back, for a few moments only, to Richmond Hill?

Counsellor Benson (or Benzon) is generally supposed to have been the last true-blue celebrity to inhabit the famous old house. He was Governor of the Danish Islands, and an eccentric. Our old friend Verplanck says that he himself dined there once with thirteen others, all speaking different languages.... "None of whom I ever saw before," he states, "but all pleasant fellows.... I, the only American, the rest of every different nation in Europe and no one the same, and all of us talking bad French together!"

It was soon after this that the city began cutting up old lots into new, and turning what had been solitary country estates into gregarious suburbs and, soon, metropolitan sections. Among other strange performances, they levelled the hills of New York - is it not odd to remember that there once were hills, many hills, in New York? And right and left they did their commissioner-like best to cut the town all to one pattern. Of course they couldn't, quite, but the effort was of lasting and painfully efficacious effect. They could not find it in their hearts, I suppose, to raze Richmond Hill House completely, - it was a noble landmark, and a home of memories which ought to have given even commissioners pause, - and maybe did. But they began to lower it - yes: take it down literally. No one with an imaginative soul can fail to feel that as they lowered the house in site and situation so they gradually but relentlessly permitted it to be lowered in character. It is with a distinct pang that I recall the steps of Richmond Hill's decline: material and spiritual, its two-sided fall appears to have kept step.

A sort of degeneracy struck the erstwhile lovely and exclusive old neighbourhood. Such gay resorts as Vauxhall and Ranelagh Gardens had encroached on the aristocratic regions of Lispenard's Meadows and their vicinity. Brannan's Gardens were close to the present crossing of Hudson and Spring streets. And - Richmond Hill did not escape! It too became a tavern, a pleasure resort, a "mead garden," a roadhouse - whatever you choose to call it. It, with its contemporaries, was the goal of many a gay party and I am told that its "turtle dinners" were incomparable! In winter there were sleighing parties, a gentleman and lady in each sleigh; and - but here is a better picture-maker than I to give it to you - one Thomas Janvier, in short:

"How brave a sight it must have been when - the halt for

refreshments being ended - the long line of carriages got under way again and went dashing along the causeway over Lispenard's green meadows, while the silvered harness of the horses and the brilliant varnish of the Italian chaises gleamed and sparkled in the rays of nearly level sunshine from the sun that was setting there a hundred years and more ago!"

The secretary and engineer to the commissioners who cut up, levelled and made over New York was John Randel, Jr., and he has left us most minute and prolific writings, covering everything he saw in the course of his work; indeed one wonders how he ever had time to work at all at his profession! Among his records is this account of dear Richmond Hill before it had been lowered to the level of the valley lands. It was, in fact, the last of the hills to go.

After describing carefully the exact route he took daily to the Commissioners' office in Greenwich, as far as Varick Street where the excavations for St. John's Church were then being made (1808), and stating that he crossed the ditch at Canal Street on a plank, he goes on thus:

"From this crossing place I followed a well-beaten path leading from the city to the then village of Greenwich, passing over open and partly fenced lots and fields, not at that time under cultivation, and remote from any dwelling-house now remembered by me except Colonel Aaron Burr's former country-seat, on elevated ground, called Richmond Hill, which was about one hundred or one hundred and fifty yards west of this path, and was then occupied as a place of refreshment for gentlemen taking a drive from the city."

In 1820, if I am not mistaken, the levelling (and lowering) process was complete. Richmond Hill's sad old windows looked no longer down upon a beautiful country world, but out on swiftly growing city blocks. In 1831, a few art-loving souls tried to found a high-class theatre in the old house, - the

Richmond Hill Theatre. Among them was Lorenzo Daponte, who had been exiled from Venice, and wrote witty satirical verse.

The little group of sincere idealists wanted this theatre to be a real home of high art, and a prize was offered for the best "poetical address on the occasion," - that is, the opening of the theatre. The judges and contestants sat in one of the historic reception rooms that had seen such august guests as Washington and Burr, Adams and Hamilton, Talleyrand and Louis Philippe.

Our good friend General Wetmore can tell us of this at first hand for he was one of those present.

"It was," he says, "an afternoon to be remembered. As the long twilight deepened into evening, the shadows of departed hosts and long-forgotten guests seemed to hover 'round the dilapidated halls and the dismantled chambers."

The winner of the prize was Fitz-Greene Halleck; and it was not at all a bad poem, though too long to quote here.

The theatre was never a brilliant success. To be sure, such sterling actors as Mr. and Mrs. John Barnes and the Hilsons played there, and during a short season of Italian opera, in which Daponte was enthusiastically interested, Adelaide Pedrotti was the prima donna. And one of New York's first "opera idols" sang there - Luciano Fornasari, generally acclaimed by New York ladies as the handsomest man who had ever been in the city! For a wonder, he wasn't a tenor, only a basso, but they adored him just the same.

Somehow it grows hard to write of Richmond Hill - a hill no longer, but a shabby playhouse, which was not even successful. The art-loving impresarios spent the little money they had very speedily and there was no more Richmond Hill Theatre.

Then a circus put up there - yes, a circus - in the same house which had made even sensible Mrs. Adams dream dreams, and where Theo Burr had entertained her Indian Chief! In 1842, it was the headquarters of a menagerie, pure and simple.

In 1849 - thank God - its nightmare of desecration was over. It was pulled down, and they built red-brick houses on its grave and left its ancient memories to sleep in peace.

> "And thus" [Wetmore once again] "passed away the glories and the shadows of Richmond Hill. All that remains of them are a few fleeting memories and a page or two of history fast fading into oblivion."

For once, I cannot quite agree with him - not when he says that. For surely the home of so much romance and grandeur and charm and importance must leave something behind it other than a few fleeting memories and a page or two of history. Houses have ghosts as well as people, and if ever there stood a house with a personality, that was sweet, poignant and indestructible, it was the House on Richmond Hill.

I, who tell you this, am very sure. Have I not seen it sketched in bright, shadowy lines upon the air above Charlton and Varick streets, - its white columns shining through all the modern city murk? Go there in the right mood and at the right moment, and you will see, too.

## CHAPTER V

## "TOM PAINE, INFIDEL."

... These are the times that try men's souls. The summer soldier and the sunshine patriot will, in this crisis, shrink from the service of their country; but he that stands it _now_, deserves the love and thanks of man and woman.... I have as little superstition in me as any man living; but my secret opinion has ever been, and still is, that God Almighty will not give up a people to military destruction, or leave them unsupportedly to perish, who have so earnestly and so repeatedly sought to avoid the calamities of war, by every decent method which wisdom could invent.

- "THE CRISIS."

I want you to note carefully the title of this chapter. And then I want you to note still more carefully the quotation with which it opens. It was the man known far and wide as "the infidel," - the man who was denounced by church-goers, and persecuted for his unorthodox doctrines, - who wrote with such high and happy confidence of a fair, a just and a merciful God Almighty.

Before me lies a letter from W.M. van der Weyde, the president of the Thomas Paine National Historical Association. One paragraph meets my eyes at this moment:

Anna Alice Chapin

"Paine was, without doubt, the very biggest figure that ever lived in 'Greenwich Village.' I think, on investigation, you will realise the truth of this statement."

I have realised it. And that is why I conceive no book on Greenwich complete without a chapter devoted to him who came to be known as "the great Commoner of Mankind." He spoke of himself as a "citizen of the world," and there are many quarters of the globe that can claim a share in his memory, so we will claim it, too!

It is true that Thomas Paine lived but a short time in Greenwich, and that the long play of his full and colourful career was enacted before he came to spend his last days in the Village. But he is none the less an essential part of Greenwich; his illustrious memory is so signal a source of pride to the neighbourhood, his personality seems still so vividly present, that his life and acts must have a place there, too. The street that was named "Reason" because of him, suggests the persecutions abroad and at home which followed the writing of that extraordinary and daring book "The Age of Reason." The name of Mme. de Bonneville, who chose for him the little frame house on the site which is now about at 59 Grove Street, recalls his dramatic life chapter in Paris, where he first met the De Bonnevilles. So, you see, one cannot write of Thomas Paine in Greenwich, without writing of Thomas Paine in the great world - working, fighting, pleading, suffering, lighting a million fires of courage and of inspiration, living so hard and fast and strenuously, that to read over his experiences, his experiments and his achievements, is like reading the biographies of a score of different busy men!

He was born of Quaker parentage, at Thetford, Norfolk, in England, on January 29, 1737, and pursued many avocations before he found his true vocation - that of a world liberator, and apostle of freedom and human rights. One of his most sympathetic commentators, H.M. Brailsford, says of him:

"His writing is of the age of enlightenment; his actions

belong to romance.... In his spirit of adventure, in his passion for movement and combat, there Paine is romantic. Paine thought in prose and acted epics. He drew horizons on paper and pursued the infinite in deeds."

Let us see where this impulse of romance and adventure led him; it was into strange enough paths at first!

He was a mere boy - fifteen or sixteen, if I remember accurately - when the lure of the sea seized him. It is reported that he signed up on a privateer (the Captain of which was appropriately called Death!), putting out from England, and sailed with her piratical crew for a year. This was doubtless adventurous enough, but young Thomas already wanted adventure of a different and a higher order. He came back and went into his Quaker father's business - which was that of a staymaker, of all things! He got his excitement by studying *astronomy!*

Then he became an exciseman - what was sometimes called "gauger" - and was speedily cashiered for negligence. Anyone may have three guesses as to his reported next ambition. More than one historian has declared that he wished to take orders in the Church of England. This is, however, extremely unlikely. In any case, he changed his mind in time, and was again taken on as exciseman. Likewise, he was again dismissed. This time they fired him for advocating higher wages and writing a pamphlet on the subject. The reform fever had caught him, you perceive, and he was nevermore free from it, to the day of his death.

He was a brilliant mathematician and an ingenious inventor. Brailsford says that his inventions were "partly useful, partly whimsical." They would be, of course. They included a crane, a planing-machine, a smokeless candle and a gunpowder motor - besides his really big and notable invention of the first iron bridge.

But that came later. Before leaving England, in addition to his other and varied occupations, he ran a "tobacco mill," and was twice married. One wife died, and from the other he was separated. At all events, at thirty-seven, alone and friendless, with empty pockets and a letter from Benjamin Franklin as his sole asset, he set sail for America in the year 1774.

Of course he went to the Quaker City, and speedily became the editor of the *Pennsylvania Magazine*, through the pages of which he cried a new message of liberty and justice to the troubled Colonies. He, an Englishman, urged America to break away from England; he, of Quaker birth and by heredity and training opposed to fighting, advocated the most stringent steps for the consummation of national freedom. In that clear-eyed and disinterested band of men who conceived and cradled our Republic, Paine stands a giant even among giants.

Many persons believe that it was he who actually composed and wrote the Declaration of Independence; it is certain that he is more than half responsible for it. The very soul and fibre and living spirit of the United States was the soul and fibre and living spirit of Thomas Paine, and, in the highest American standards and traditions, remains the same today.

In 1775 he wrote "Common Sense" - the book which was, as one historian declares, the "clarion call for separation from England," and which swept the country. Edmund Randolph drily ascribes American independence first to George III and second to Paine. Five hundred thousand copies of the pamphlet were sold, and he might easily have grown rich on the proceeds, but he could never find it in his conscience to make money out of patriotism, and he gave every cent to the war fund.

This splendid fire-eating Quaker - is there anything stauncher than a fighting Quaker? - proceeded to enlist in the Pennsylvania division of the Flying Camp under General Roberdeau; then he went as aide-de-camp to General Greene. It was in 1776 that he started his "Crisis," a series of stirring and patriotic addresses in pamphlet form. General Washington ordered the first copy read aloud to every regiment in the Continental Army, and its effect is now history.

Ella Wheeler Wilcox has written of this:

> "... Many of the soldiers were shoeless and left bloody footprints on the snow-covered line of march. All were but half-hearted at this time and many utterly discouraged. Washington wrote most apprehensively concerning the situation to the Congress. Paine, in the meantime (himself a soldier, with General Greene's army on the retreat from Fort Lee, New Jersey, to Newark), realising the necessity of at once instilling renewed hope and courage in the soldiers if the cause of liberty was to be saved, wrote by campfire at night the first number of his soul-stirring 'Crisis.'"

It was before Trenton that those weary and disheartened soldiers, - ragged, barefoot, half frozen and more than half starved - first heard the words that have echoed down the years:

> *"These are the times that try men's souls!"*

They answered that call; every man of them answered Paine's heart cry, as they took up their muskets again. It was with that immortal sentence as a war slogan, that the Battle of Trenton was won.

Is it any wonder that in England the "Crisis" was ordered to be burned by the hangman? It was a more formidable enemy than anything ever devised in the shape of steel or powder!

A list of Paine's services to this country would be too long to set down here. The Association dedicated to his memory and honour cites twenty-four important reasons why he stands among the very first and noblest figures in American history. And there are dozens more that they don't cite. He did things that were against possibility. When the patriot cause was weak for lack of money he gave a year's salary to start a bank to finance the army, and coaxed, commanded and hypnotised other people into subscribing enough to carry it. He went to Paris and induced the French King to give $6,000,000 to American independence. He wrote "Rights of Man" and the "Age of Reason," - and, incidentally, was outlawed in England and imprisoned in France! He did more and received less compensation for what he did, either in worldly goods or in gratitude, than any figure in relatively recent history.

America, though - I hear you say! - America, for whom he fought and laboured and sacrificed himself: she surely appreciated his efforts? Listen. On his return from Europe, America disfranchised him, ostracised him and repudiated him, refusing, among other indignities, to let him ride in public coaches.

So be it. He is not the first great man who has found the world thankless. Oddly enough, it troubled him little in comparison with the satisfaction he felt in seeing his exalted projects meet with success. So that good things were effectually accomplished, he cared not a whit who got the credit.

In reference to the charges against him of being "an infidel," or guilty of "infidelity," he himself, with that straightforward and happy confidence which made some men call him a braggart, wrote:

> "They have not yet accused Providence of Infidelity. Yet, according to their outrageous piety, she (Providence) must be as bad as Thomas Paine; she has protected him in all his dangers, patronised him in all his undertakings, encouraged him in all his ways...."

It is true, as Mr. van der Weyde points out in an article in *The Truth Seeker* (N.Y.), that a most extraordinary and beneficent luck, - or was it rather a guardian angel? - stood guard over Paine. His narrow escapes from death would make a small book in themselves. I will only mention one here.

During his imprisonment in the Luxembourg Prison in Paris, Thomas Paine was one of the many who were sentenced to be guillotined at that period when the moral temperature of France was many degrees above the normal mark, and men doled out death more freely than *sous*. It was the custom among the jailers to make a chalk mark upon the door of each cell that held a man condemned. Paine was one of a "consignment" of one hundred and sixty-eight prisoners sentenced to be beheaded at dawn, and the jailer made the fateful chalk mark upon his door along with the others, that the guards would know he was destined for the tumbrel that rolled away from the prison hour by hour all through the night. *But his door chanced to be open*, so that the mark, hastily made, turned out to be on the wrong side! When the door was closed it was inside, and no one knew of it; so the guard passed on, and Paine lived.

It is interesting but difficult to write about Thomas Paine.

The trouble about him is that his personality is too overwhelming to be cut and measured in proper lengths by any writer. He does not lend himself, like lesser historical figures, to continuous or disinterested narrative. The authors who have been rash enough to try to tell something about him can no more pick and choose the incidents of his career that will make the most effective "stuff" than they could reduce the phenomena of a cyclone or the aurora borealis to a consistent narrative form.

Thus: One starts to speak of Paine's experiences in Paris, and brings up in New Rochelle; one endeavours to anchor him in Greenwich, only to find oneself trailing his weary but stubborn footsteps in the war! And always and forever, Paine himself persists in crowding out the legitimate sequence of his adventures. No one can soberly write the story of his life; one can, at best, only achieve a diatribe or an apotheosis!

Anna Alice Chapin

Said he:

"The sun needs no inscription to distinguish him from darkness."

This quotation might almost serve as a text for the life of Paine, might it not? And yet - there are people in the world who wear smoked glasses, through which, I imagine, the sun himself looks not unlike a muddy splash of yellow paint upon the heavens!

This is a book about Greenwich Village and not a defence of Thomas Paine. Yet, since the reader has come with me thus far, I am going to take advantage of his courteous attention for just another moment of digression. Here is my promise: that it shall take up a small, small space.

Small insects sting dangerously; and on occasion, a very trivial and ill-considered word or phrase will cling closer and longer than a serious or thoughtful judgment. When Theodore Roosevelt called Thomas Paine "a filthy little Atheist" (or was the adjective "dirty"? I really forget!) he was very young, - only twenty-eight, - and doubtless had accepted his viewpoint of the great reformer-patriot from that "hearsay upon hearsay" against which Paine himself has so urgently warned us. Of course Mr. Roosevelt, who is both intellectual and broad-minded, knows better than that today. But it is astonishing how that ridiculous and unsuitable epithet - (a "trinity of lies" as one historian has styled it) - has stuck to a memory which I am sure is sacred to any angels who may be in heaven!

"Atheist" is a word which could be applied to few men less suitably than to Paine. From first to last, he preached the goodness of God, the power of God, the justice and mercy and infallibility of God; and he lived in a profound trust in and love for God, and a hopeful and courageous effort to carry out such principles of moral and national right-doing as he believed to be the will of his beloved Creator.

"If this," as one indignant enthusiast exclaimed, "is to be an Atheist, then Jesus Christ must have been an Atheist!"

As incongruous as anything else, in the judgment of Paine, is the fact that he has, apparently, been adopted by the pacifists. The pacifists and - Paine! - Paine who never in all his seventy years was out of a scrap! They could scarcely have chosen a less singularly unfit guiding star, for Paine was a confirmed fighter for anything and everything he held right. And his militancy was not merely of action but of the soul, not only of policy or necessity but of spiritual conviction. When even Washington was inclined to submit patiently a bit longer, it was Paine who lashed America into righteous war. He fought for the freedom of the country, for the abolition of slavery, for the rights of women; he fought for old-age pensions, for free public schools, for the protection of dumb animals, for international copyright; for a hundred and one ideals of equity and humanity which today are legislature. And he fought with his body and his brain; with his "flaming eloquence" and also with a gun! Once let him perceive the cause to be a just one, and - I know of no more magnificently belligerent a figure in all history.

And yet note here the splendid, the illuminating paradox: Paine abhorred war. Every truly great fighter has abhorred war, else he were not truly great. In 1778, in the very thick of the Revolution, he wrote solemnly:

"If there is a sin superior to every other, it is that of wilful and offensive war.... He who is the author of a war lets loose the whole contagion of hell, and opens a vein that bleeds a nation to death." (A copy of this, together with the President's recent message, might advantageously be sent to a certain well-known address on the other side of the world!) Yet did Paine, with this solemn horror of war, suggest that the United States stop fighting? No more than he had suggested that they keep out of trouble in the first place. Paine hated war in itself; but he held war a proper and righteous means to noble ends.

Anna Alice Chapin

Consistency is not only the bugbear of little minds; it is also the trade-mark of them. Paine also detested monarchies. "Some talent is required to be a simple workman," he wrote; "to be a king there is need to have only the human shape." Of Burke, he said: "Mr. Burke's mind is above the homely sorrows of the vulgar. He can feel only for a king or a queen.... He pities the plumage, but forgets the dying bird."

Yet when he was a member of that French Assembly that voted King Louis to death, he fought the others fiercely, - even though unable to speak French, - persistently opposing them, with a passionate determination and courage which came near to costing him his life. For, as Brailsford says, "The Terror made mercy a traitor."

Are these things truly paradoxes, or are they rather manifestations of that God-given reason which can clearly see things as they are as well as things as they should be, and see both to good and helpful purpose?

In 1802 Paine returned to America, just sixty-five years old. He had suffered terribly, had rendered great services and it was at least reasonable that he should expect a welcome. What happened is tersely told by Rufus Rockwell Wilson:

"When, at the age of sixty-five, he came again to the nation he had helped to create, he was met by the new faces of a generation that knew him not, and by the cold shoulders, instead of the outstretched hands, of old friends. This was the bitter fruit of his 'Age of Reason,' which remains of all epoch-making books the one most persistently misquoted and misunderstood; for even now there are those who rate it as scoffing and scurrilous, whereas its tone throughout is noble and reverent, and some of the doctrines which it teaches are now recognised as not inimical to religion."

Brailsford, of a more picturesque turn of phrase, says that "slave-owners, ex-royalists, and the fanatics of orthodoxy" were against him, and adds:

> "... The grandsons of the Puritan Colonists who had flogged Quaker women as witches denied him a place on the stage-coach, lest an offended God should strike it with lightning."

The state of New York, in a really surprising burst of generosity, presented him a farm in New Rochelle, and then, lest he imagine the Government too grateful, took away his right to vote there. They offered the flimsy excuse that he was a French citizen, - which, of course, he wasn't, - but it was all part of the persecution inspired by organised bigotry and the resentful conservative interests which he had so long and so unflaggingly attacked.

And so at last to Greenwich Village! Though I cannot engage that we shall not step out of it before we are through.

Thomas Paine was old and weary with his arduous and honourable years when he came to live in the little frame house on Herring Street, kept by one Mrs. Ryder.

John Randel, Jr., engineer to the Commissioners who were at work re-cutting New York, has given us this picture of Paine:

> "I boarded in the city, and in going to the office almost daily passed the house in Herring Street" [now No. 309 Bleecker Street] "where Thomas Paine resided, and frequently in fair weather saw him sitting at the south window of the first-story room of that house. The sash was raised, and a small table or stand was placed before him with an open book upon it which he appeared to be reading. He had his spectacles on, his left elbow rested upon the table or stand, and his chin rested between thumb and fingers of his hand; his right hand lay upon his book, and a decanter next his book or beyond it. I never saw Thomas Paine at any other place or in any other position."

In this house Paine was at one time desperately ill. It was said that the collapse was partly due to his too sudden abstinence from stimulants. He was an old man then, and had lived with every ounce of energy that was in him. The stimulants were resumed, and he grew somewhat better. This naturally brings us to the question of Paine as an excessive drinker. Of course people said he was; but then people said he was a great many things that he was not. When his enemies grew tired of the monotony of crying "Tom Paine, the infidel," they cried "Tom Paine, the drunkard" instead.

Which recalls a story which is an old one but too applicable not to be quoted here.

It is said that some official - and officious - mischief-maker once came to Lincoln with the report that one of the greatest and most distinguished of Federal generals was in the habit of drinking too much.

"Indeed?" said Lincoln drily. "If that is true, I should like to send a barrel of the same spirits to some of my other generals."

If Thomas Paine did drink to excess - which seems extremely doubtful - it's a frightful and solemn argument against Prohibition!

Mrs. Ryder's house where Paine lived was close to that occupied by his faithful friend Mme. de Bonneville and her two sons. Paine was devoted to the boys, indeed the younger was named for him, and their visits were among his greatest pleasures. And, by the bye, while we are on the subject, the most scurrilous and unjust report ever circulated against this great man was that which cast a reflection upon the honourable and kindly relations existing between him and Mme. de Bonneville.

In the first place, Paine had never been a man of light or loose morals, and it is scarcely likely that he should have changed his entire character at the age of three score and ten. Mme. de

Bonneville's husband, Nicholas, was a close friend of Paine in Paris, and had originally intended to come to America with Paine and his family. But, as the publisher of a highly Radical paper - the *Bien Informe* - De Bonneville was under espionage, and when the time came he was not permitted to leave France. He confided his wife and children to his friend, and they set sail with his promise to follow later. He did follow, when he could - Washington Irving tells of chatting with him in Battery Park - but it was too late for him to see the man who had proved himself so true a friend to him and his.

The older De Bonneville boy was Benjamin, known affectionately by his parents and Paine as "Bebia." He was destined to become distinguished in the Civil War - Gen. Benjamin de Bonneville, of high military and patriotic honours.

I said we couldn't keep to Greenwich - we have travelled to France and back again already!

You may find the house if you care to look for it - the very same house kept by Mrs. Ryder, where Thomas Paine lived more than a century ago. So humble and shabby it is you might pass it by with no more notice than you would pass a humble and shabby wayfarer. Its age and picturesqueness do not arrest the eye; for it isn't the sort of old house which by quaint lines and old-world atmosphere tempt the average artist or lure the casual poet to its praise. It is just a little old wooden building of another day, where people of modest means were wont to live.

The caretaker there probably does not know anything about the august memory that with him inhabits the dilapidated rooms. He doubtless fails to appreciate the honour of placing his hand upon the selfsame polished mahogany stair rail which our immortal "infidel's" hand once pressed, or the rare distinction of reading his evening paper at the selfsame window where, with his head upon his hand, that Other was wont to read too, once upon a time.

Ugly, dingy rooms they are in that house, but glorified by association. There is, incidentally, a mantelpiece which anyone might envy, though now buried in barbarian paint. There are gable windows peering out from the shingled roof.

Some day the Thomas Paine Association will probably buy it, undertake the long-forgotten national obligation, and prevent it from crumbling to dust as long as ever they can.

The caretaker keeps pets - cats and kittens and dogs and puppies. Once he kept pigeons too, but the authorities disapproved, he told me.

"Ah, well," I said, "the authorities never have approved of things in this house."

He thought me quite mad.

Let us walk down the street toward that delicious splash of green - like a verdant spray thrown up from some unseen river of trees. There is, in reality, no river of trees; it is only Christopher Street Triangle, elbowing Sheridan Square. Subway construction is going on around us, but there clings still an old-world feeling. Ah, here we are - 59 Grove Street. It is a modest but a charming little red-brick house with a brass knocker and an air of unpretentious, small-scale prosperity. It has only been built during the last half-century, but it stands on the identical plot of ground where Paine's other Greenwich residence once stood. It wasn't Grove Street then; in fact, it wasn't a street at all, but an open lot with one lone frame house in the middle of it. Here Mme. de Bonneville brought Thomas Paine when his age and ill health necessitated greater comforts than Mrs. Ryder's lodgings could afford.

Here he spent some peaceful months with only a few visitors; but those were faithful ones. One was Willett Hicks, the Quaker preacher, always a staunch friend; another was John Wesley Jarvis, the American painter - the same artist who later made the great man's death mask.

It was Jarvis who said: "He devoted his whole life to the attainment of two objects - rights of man and freedom of conscience."

And, by the bye, Dr. Conway has declared that "his 'Rights of Man' is now the political constitution of England, his 'Age of Reason' is the growing constitution of its Church."

In passing I must once again quote Mr. van der Weyde, who once said to me: "I often wonder just what share Mary Wollstonecraft had with her 'Rights of Women' - in the inspiration of Paine's 'Rights of Man.' He and she, you know, were close friends."

Another friend was Robert Fulton of steamboat fame. I have truly heard Paine enthusiasts declare that our "infidel" was the authentic inventor of the steamboat! In any case, he is known to have "palled" with Fulton, and certainly gave him many ideas.

There were, to be sure, annoyances. He was, in spite of Mme. de Bonneville's affectionate protection, still an object of persecution.

Two clergymen were especially tireless in their desire to reform this sterling reformer. I believe their names were Milledollar and Cunningham. Janvier tells this anecdote:

> "It was during Paine's last days in the little house in Greenwich that two worthy divines, the Rev. Mr. Milledollar and the Rev. Mr. Cunningham, sought to bring him to a realising sense of the error of his ways. Their visitation was not a success. 'Don't let 'em come here again,' he said, curtly, to his housekeeper, Mrs. Hedden, when they had departed; and added: 'They trouble me.' In pursuance of this order, when they returned to the attack, Mrs. Hedden denied them admission - saying with a good deal of piety, and with even more common-sense: 'If God does not change his

mind, I'm sure no man can!'"

Apropos of the two houses occupied by Paine in our city Mr. van der Weyde has pointed out most interestingly the striking and almost miraculous way in which they have just escaped destruction. Paine's "Providence" has seemed to stand guard over the places sacred to him, just as it stood guard over his invaluable life. A dozen times 309 Bleecker Street and 59 Grove Street have almost gone in the relentless constructive demolition of metropolitan growth and progress. But - they have not gone yet!

I have said that the Grove Street house stood in an open lot, the centre of a block at that time. Just after Paine's death a street was cut through, called Cozine Street. Names were fleeting affairs in early and fast-growing New York, and the one street from Cozine became Columbia, then Burrows, and last of all Grove, which it remains today.

Here let us make a note of one more indignity which the officially wise and virtuous ones were able to bestow upon their unassumingly wise and virtuous victim.

The Commissioners replanning New York desired to pay Paine's memory a compliment and on opening up the street parallel with Grove, they called it Reason Street, for the "Age of Reason." This was objected to by many bigots (who had never read the book) and some tactful diplomat suggested giving it the French twist - *Raison* Street. Already they had the notion that French could cover a multitude of sins. Even this was too closely suggestive of Tom Paine, "the infidel," so it was shamelessly corrupted to Raisin! Consider the street named originally in honour of the author of the "Age of Reason," eventually called for a dried grape!

This too passed, and if you go down there now you will find it called Barrow Street.

On the 8th of June, 1809, Thomas Paine died.

The New York *Advertiser* said:

> "With heart-felt sorrow and poignant regret, we are compelled to announce to the world that Thomas Paine is no more. This distinguished philanthropist, whose life was devoted to the cause of humanity, departed this life yesterday morning; and, if any man's memory deserves a place in the breast of a freeman, it is that of the deceased, for,
>
> *"'Take him for all in all,*
> *We ne'er shall look upon his like again.'"*

The funeral party consisted of Hicks, Mme. de Bonneville and two negroes, who loyally walked twenty-two miles to New Rochelle to see the last of the man who had always defended and pleaded for the rights of their pitifully misunderstood and ill-treated race.

To the end he was active for public service. His actual last act was to pen a letter to the Federal faction, conveying a warning as to the then unsettled situation in American and French commerce. Just before he had made his will.

It is in itself a composition worth copying and preserving. Paine could not even execute a legal document without putting into it something of the beauty of spirit and distinction of phrase for which he was remarkable. He had not much to leave, since he had given all to his country and his country had forgotten him in making up the balance; but what he had went to Mme. de Bonneville, for her children, that she, - let me quote his own words, "... might bring them well up, give them good and useful learning and instruct them in their duty to God and the practice of morality."

It continues thus:

> "I herewith take my final leave of them and the world. I have lived an honest and useful life to mankind; my time

has been spent in doing good and I die in perfect composure and resignation to the will of my Creator God."

Such was the last will and testament of "Tom Paine, Infidel."

# CHAPTER VI

## PAGES OF ROMANCE

In the resolute spirit of another Andor Andorra, the Village of Greenwich maintains its independence in the very midst of the city of New York - submitting to no more of a compromise in the matter of its autonomy than is evolved in the Procrustean sort of splicing which has hitched fast the extremities of its tangled streets to the most readily available streets in the City Plan. The flippant carelessness with which this apparent union has been effected only serves to emphasise the actual separation. In almost every case these ill-advised couplings are productive of anomalous disorder, which in the case of the numbered streets they openly travesty the requirements of communal propriety and of common-sense: as may be inferred from the fact that within this disjointed region Fourth Street crosses Tenth, Eleventh and Twelfth streets very nearly at right angles - to the permanent bewilderment of nations and to the perennial confusion of mankind.

- THOMAS JANVIER.

It seems a far cry from the Greenwich of the last century to the Greenwich of this; from such quaint, garden-enclosed houses as the Warren homestead and Richmond Hill, from the alternately adventurous and tranquil lives of the great men who used to walk its crooked streets long and long ago, to the Studio quarter of today. What tie between the Grapevine, Vauxhall, Ranelagh, Brannan's, and all the ancient hostelries and mead houses and the modern French and Italian restaurants and little tea shops which are part and parcel of the present Village? So big did the gap appear to your servant, the author, so incongruous the notion of uniting the old and the new Greenwich harmoniously that she was close to giving the problem up in despair and writing her story of Greenwich Village in two books instead of one. But - whether accidentally or by inspiration, who knows? - three sovereign bonds became accidentally plain to her. May they be as plain to you who read - bonds between the Green Village of an older day and the Bohemian Village of this our own day, points that the old and the new settlements have in common - more - points that show the soul and spirit of the Village to be one and the same, unchanged in the past, unchanged in the present, probably to be unchanged for all time. The first of these points I have already touched upon in an earlier chapter - the deathless element of romance that has always had its headquarters here. Every city, like every brain, should have a corner given over to dreams. Greenwich is the dream-corner of New York. Everyone feels it. I found an old article in the *Tribune* written by Vincent Pepe which shows how the romance of the neighbourhood has crept into bricks and stone and even the uncompromising prose of real estate.

"Each one of these houses in the Village is from seventy-five to one hundred years old," writes Mr. Pepe (he might have said a hundred and fifty with equal accuracy in a few cases), "and each one of them has a history of its own, individually, as being one of the houses occupied by someone who has made American history and some of these houses have produced some of our present great men.

"New York has nothing of the old, with the exception of those old Colonial houses and for this reason we are trying to preserve them.... This is the great advantage and distinction of Washington Square and Greenwich Village and this is what has made it popular and it will be greater as the years go by. It will improve more and more with age, like an old wine.

"There is only one old section of New York and that is Greenwich Village and Washington Square, and the public are also going to preserve this little part of old New York."

Then there is that curious quality about Greenwich so endearing to those who know it, the quality of a haven, a refuge, a place of protected freedom.

"It's a good thing," said a certain brilliant young writer-man to me, "that there's one place where you can be yourself, live as you will and work out your scheme of life without a lot of criticism and convention to keep tripping you up. The point of view of the average mortal - out in the city - is that if you don't do exactly as everyone else does there's something the matter with you, morally or mentally. In the Village they leave you in peace, and take it for granted that you're decent until you've blatantly proven yourself the opposite. I'd have lost my nerve or my wits or my balance or something if I hadn't had the Village to come and *breathe* in!"

Not so different from the reputation of Old Greenwich, is it? - a place where the rich would be healed, the weary rest and the sorrowful gain comfort. Not so different from the lure that drew Sir. Peter out to the Green Village between his spectacular and hazardous voyages; that gave Thomas Paine his "seven serene months" before death came to him; that filled the grassy lanes with a mushroom business-life which had fled before the scourge of yellow fever; not so different from the refreshing ease of heart that came to Abigail Adams and Theodosia Alston when they came there from less comforting atmospheres. Greenwich, you see, maintains its old and honourable repute - that of being a resort and shelter and refuge for those upon whom the world outside would have pressed too heavily.

There is no one who has caught the inconsequent, yet perfectly sincere spirit of the Village better than John Reed. In reckless, scholarly rhyme he has imprisoned something of the reckless idealism of the Artists' Quarter - that haven for unconventional souls.

> *"Yet we are free who live in Washington Square,*
> *We dare to think as uptown wouldn't dare,*
> *Blazing our nights with arguments uproarious;*
> *What care we for a dull old world censorious,*
> *When each is sure he'll fashion something glorious?"*

So we find that the romance of Colonial days still blooms freshly below Fourteenth Street and that people still rush to the Village to escape the world and its ways as eagerly as they fled a hundred years ago. But the third and last point of unity is perhaps the most striking. Always, we know, Greenwich has refused rebelliously to conform to any rule of thumb. We know that when the Commissioners checker-boarded off the town they found they couldn't checker-board Greenwich. It was too independent and too set in its ways. It had its lanes and trails and cow-paths and nothing could induce it to become resigned to straight streets and measured avenues. It would not conform, and it never has conformed. And even more strenuously has its mental development defied the draughtsman's compass and triangle. Greenwich will not straighten its streets nor conventionalise its views. Its intellectual conclusions will always be just as unexpected as the squares and street angles that one stumbles on head first. Its habit of life will be just as weirdly individual as its tangled blocks. It asks nothing better than to be let alone. It does not welcome tourists, though it is hospitality itself to wayfarers seeking an open door. It is the Village, and it will never, never, no *never* be anything else - the Village of the streets that wouldn't be straight!

Janvier, who has already been quoted extensively, but who has written of Greenwich so well that his quotations can't be avoided, says: "In addition to being hopelessly at odds with the surrounding city, Greenwich is handsomely at variance with itself."

New York, and especially Greenwich, grew by curious and indirect means, as we have seen. This fact and a lively and sympathetic consciousness of it, leads often to seemingly irrelevant digressions. Yet, is it not worth a moment's pause to find out that the stately site of Washington Square North, as well as other adjacent and select territory, was originally the property of two visionary seamen; and that the present erratic deflection of Broadway came from one obstinate Dutchman's affection for his own grounds and his uncompromising determination to use a gun to defend them, even against a city?

So, lest what follows appears to be a digression or an irrelevance, let me venture to remind you that the Village has always grown not only with picturesque results but by picturesque methods and through picturesque mediums. It is frankly, incurably romantic. Sir. Peter Warren's estates, or part of them, were sold off in parcels by the fine old custom of dice-throwing. Here is the official record of that episode, by the bye:

> "In pursuance of the powers given in the said antenuptial deeds the trustees therein named, on March 31, 1787, agreed upon a partition of the said lands, which agreement was with the approbation and consent of the cestui que trusts, to wit: Earl and Lady Abingdon, and Charles Fitsroy and Ann his wife, the said Susannah Skinner the second not then having arrived at age. In making the partition, the premises were divided into three parts on a survey made thereof and marked A, B and C; and it was agreed that such partition should be made by each of the trustees naming a person to throw dice for and in behalf of their respective cestui que trusts, and that the person who should throw the highest number should have parcel A; the one who should throw the next highest

number parcel B; and the one who should throw the lowest number, parcel C, - for the persons whom they respectively represented; and the premises were partitioned accordingly. '

Eleventh Street was never cut through because old Burgher Brevoort did not want his trees cut down and argued conclusively with a blunderbuss to that effect - a final effect. It never has been cut through, as a matter of fact, to this day. And by way of evening things up, Grace Church, which stands almost on the disputed site, had for architect one James Renwick, who married the only daughter of Henry Brevoort himself. So by a queer twisted sort of law of compensation, the city gained rather than lost by what a certain disgruntled historian calls the "obstinacy of one Dutch householder."

These things are all true; the most amazing thing about Greenwich Village is that the most unlikely things that you can find out about it are true. The obvious, every-day things that are easily believed are much the most likely to be untenable reports or the day dreams of imaginative chroniclers. You are safe if you believe all the quaint and romantic and inconsistent and impossible things that come to your knowledge concerning the Village. That is its special and sacred privilege: to be unexpected and always - yes, always without exception - in the spirit of its irrational and sympathetic role. It needs Kipling's ambiguous "And when the thing that couldn't has occurred" for a motto. And yet - and yet - like all true nonsense, this nonsense is rooted in a beautiful and disconcerting compromise of truth.

Cities do grow through their romances and their adventures. The commonplaces of life never opened up new worlds nor established them after; the prose of life never served as a song of progress. Never a great onward movement but was called impossible. The things that the sane-and-safe gentleman accepts as good sense are not the things that make for growth, anywhere. And the principle, applied to lesser things, holds good. Who wants to study a city's life through the registries of its civic diseases or cures? We want its romances, its exceptions, its absurdities, its adventures. We not only want them, we must have them. Despite all the wiseacres on earth we care more for the duel that Burr and Hamilton fought than for all their individual achievements, good or bad. It is the theatrical change from the Potter's Field to the centre of fashion that first catches our fancy in the tale of Washington Square. In fact, my friend, we are, first and last, children addicted to the mad yet harmless passion of story-telling and story-hearing. I do hope that, when you read these pages, you will remember that, and be not too stern in criticism of sundry vastly important historic points which are all forgot and left out of the scheme - asking your pardon!

The Village, old or new, is the home of romance (as we have said, it is to be feared at least once or twice too often ere this) and it is for us to follow those sweet and crazy trails where they may chance to lead.

Since, then, we are concerned chiefly with the spirit of adventure, we can hardly fail to note that this particular element has haunted the neighbourhood of Washington Square fairly consistently.

If you will look at the Ratzer map you will see that the Elliott estate adjoined the Brevoort lands. It is today one of the most variously important regions in town, embracing as it does both Broadway and Fifth Avenue and including a most lively business section and a most exclusive aristocratic quarter. Andrew Elliott was the son of Sir. Gilbert Elliott, Lord Chief Justice, Clerk of Scotland. Andrew was Receiver General of the Province of New York under the Crown and a most loyal Royalist to the last. When the British rule passed he, in common with many other English sympathisers, found himself in an embarrassing position. The De Lanceys - close friends of his - lost their lands outright. But Elliott, like the canny Scotchman that he was, was determined that he would not be served the same way.

To quote Mr. J.H. Henry, who now handles that huge property: "He must have had friends! Apparently they liked him, if they didn't like his politics."

This is how they managed it: He transferred his entire estate to a Quaker friend of his in Philadelphia - this was before the situation had become too critical; then a little group of friendly New Yorkers, among whom was Alexander Hamilton, bought it in; next it passed into the hands of one Friedrich Charles Hans Bruno, Baron Poelnitz, who appears to have been not much more than a figurehead. However, it was legally his property at the time of the adoption of the Constitution of the United States, and so it was not confiscated. It probably is safe to assume that Mr. Andrew Elliott still remained the power behind the throne, and benefited by the subsequent sale of the land to Capt. Robert Richard Randall.

Which brings us to a most picturesque page of New York history.

I wonder what there is about privateering that attracts even the most law-abiding imagination. This ancient, more than half dishonourable, profession has an unholy glamour about it and there are few respectable callings that so appeal to the colour-loving fancy. Not that privateering was quite the same as piracy, but it came so close a second that the honest rogues who plied the two trades must often have been in danger of getting their perquisites and obligations somewhat merged. It would have taken a very sharp judicial mind, or a singularly stout personal conscience, to make the distinctions between them in sundry and fairly numerous cases.

Wilson says:

"In these troublous and not over-squeamish times, when commerce was other than the peaceful pursuit it has since become, a promising venture in privateering was often preferred to slower if safer sources of profit by the strong-stomached merchants and mariners of New York.... News that piracy under the guise of privateering was winked at by the New York authorities spread quickly among the captains serving under the black flag."

Now there never was a lustier freebooter of the high seas than Capt. Thomas Randall, known familiarly as "Cap'n Tom," commander of the privateering ship *Fox*, and numerous other vessels. This boat, a brigantine, was well named, for she was quick and sly and yet could fight on occasion. Many a rich haul he made in her in 1748, and many a hairbreadth escape shaved the impudent bow of her on those jolly, nefarious voyages of hers. One of her biggest captures was the French ship *L'Amazone*. In 1757 he took out the *De Lancey*, a brigantine, with fourteen guns, and made some more sensational captures. He is said to have plied a coastwise trade for the most part from New York to New Orleans, but, to quote Mr. Henry once more, "The Captain went wherever the Spanish flag covered the largest amount of gold." At all events he amassed a prodigious fortune even for a privateer. In 1758 he withdrew from active service himself, but still sent out privateering vessels. Some of them he lost. The *De Lancey* was captured, and so was the *Saucy Sally* - the latter by the British ship *Experiment*. The *De Lancey* however made some excellent hauls first. Peter Johnson, a seaman, made a will in 1757, leaving to a friend all debts, dues and "prize money which may become payable by the cruise of the *De Lancey*, Captain Randall commanding." The luckless *De Lancey* was taken by the Dutch off Curacoa and the crew imprisoned. Perhaps poor Johnson was one of them.

In spite of occasional ill-luck these were good days for the Captain, because the law, never over scrupulous, allowed him especial license, the country being at war. Never was there a better era for adventurers, never a time when fortunes were to be sought under more favourable stars!

A third quotation from Mr. Henry:

"In those days a man was looked upon as being highly

Anna Alice Chapin

unfortunate if he had not a vessel which he could put to profitable use!"

He was part owner of the *Snow* with sixteen guns, full owner of the *Mary* and also of the *Lively*. He had a bad time in connection with the latter. He sent her out with Thomas Quigley for captain. Quigley took the little schooner down the Jersey coast and stayed there. He never put out to sea at all. He rode comfortably at anchor near shore and when he ran out of rum put in and got more. After a while the mates and crew sent in a round robin to Captain Randall telling him the story. The *Lively* was swiftly called in and - what Captain Tom did to Quigley history does not state!

The jolly piratical seaman did finely and flourished, green-bay like, in the sight of men. He was not without honours either. When Washington was rowed from Elizabethtown Point to the first inauguration, his barge was manned by a crew of thirteen ships' captains, and he who had the signal distinction of being coxswain of that historic boat's company, was Cap'n Tom!

Indeed there seems to be abundant proof that the Captain engineered the whole proceeding. It is certain that it was he who presented the "Presidential barge" to Washington for his use during his stay in New York, and he who selected that unusual crew, - practically every noted shipmaster then in port. On the President's final departure for Mount Vernon, he again used the barge, putting out from the foot of Whitehall and when he reached Elizabethtown, he very courteously returned it as a gift to Captain Randall, and wrote him a letter of warm thanks.

It is believed that Captain Thomas came from Scotland some time in the early part of the eighteenth century, but we know nothing of his antecedents and not much of his private life. He married in America, but we do not know the name of his wife. We do know that in 1775 his son, Robert Richard, was a youth of nineteen and a student at Columbia. This was the same year that the old Captain was serving on important committees and playing a conspicuous part in public affairs. Oh, yes! he was a most eminent citizen, and no one thought a whit the worse of him for what he called his "honest privateering." He was a member of the Legislature in 1784 and voted in favour of bringing in tea free - when it was carried by American ships!

And I picture Cap'n Tom as a stout and hearty rogue, with an open hand and heart and a certain cheery fashion of plying his shady calling, rather endearing than otherwise (I have no notion of his real looks nor qualities, but one's imagination must have its fling on occasion!). After all, there is not such a vast difference between the manner of Sir. Peter Warren's gains and Cap'n Tom Randall's. You may call a thing by one name or by another, but, when it comes down to it, is the business of capturing enemy prize ships in order to grow rich on the proceeds so different from holding up merchantmen for the same reason? But we are concerned for the moment with the Randalls, father and son, and most excellent fellows they appear to have both been. I should like to believe that Cap'n Tom owned a cutlass, but I fear it was a bit late for that!

Captain Tom appears to have been generous and kindly, - like most persons of questionable and picturesque careers. The Silversmith who left his entire belongings to the Captain in 1796 is but one of many who had reason to love him. One historian declares that he settled down, after retiring from the sea, and "became a respectable merchant at 10 Hanover Street," where he piled up more and more gold to leave his son Robert Richard. But it is a matter of record that the address at which he died was 8 Whitehall. On Friday, October 27, 1797, he set forth on his last cruise, - after seventy-four adventurous years on earthly seas.

He died much respected, - by no one more than his son, Robert Richard Randall, who had an immense admiration and reverence for his memory. It was he who, in 1790, bought the Elliott estate from "Baron" Poelnitz, for the sum of five thousand pounds - a handsome property of some twenty-four acres covering the space between Fourth and Fifth avenues, Waverly Place and approximately Ninth Street. The Elliott house which has been described as being of "red brick with white" was clearly a rather pretentious affair, and stood, says Mrs. Lamb, so that Broadway when it was laid down "clipped the rear porch."

It is a curious fact and worthy of note that the old, original house stood undamaged until 1828, and that, being sold at auction and removed at that date, its materials were used in a house which a few years ago was still in good condition.

Robert Richard Randall was also, like his father, known as "Captain," though there is no record of his ever having gone to sea as a sailor. Indeed he would scarcely have been made an "honourary" member of the Marine Society had he been a real shipmaster. Courtesy titles were *de rigueur* in those days, when a man was popular, and he appears to have been thoroughly so.

When it came time for him, too, to die, he paid his father's calling what tribute he could by the terms of his will.

His lawyer - no less a person that Alexander Hamilton himself - called to discuss the terms of this last document. By the bye, Hamilton's part in the affair is traditional and legendary rather than a matter of official record; - certainly his name does not appear in connection with the will. But Hamilton was the lawyer of Randall's sister, and a close family friend, so the story may more easily be true than false.

This, then, is the way it goes: Alexander Hamilton was summoned to make out the last will and testament, or at least, to advise concerning it. Randall was already growing weak, but had a clear and determined notion of what he wanted to do with his money. This was on June 1, 1801. The dying man left a number of small bequests to friends, families and servants, before he came to the real business on his mind. His bequests, besides money, included, "unto Betsey Hart, my housekeeper, my gold sleeve buttons," and "unto Adam Shields, my faithful overseer, my gold watch," and "unto Gawn Irwin, who now lives with me, my shoe-buckles and knee-buckles." Adam Shields married Betsey Hart. They were both Scotch - probably from whatever part of Scotland the Randalls hailed in the first place.

When these matters were disposed of, he began to speak of what was nearest his heart. He had a good deal of money; he wanted to leave it to some lasting use. Hamilton asked how he had made his money, and Randall explained he had inherited it from his father.

"And how did he get it?" asked the great lawyer.

"By honest privateering!" declared Captain Tom's son proudly.

And then, or so the story goes, he went on to whisper:

"My father's fortune all came from the sea. He was a seaman, and a good one. He had money, so he never suffered when he was worn out, but all are not like that. I want to make a place for the others. I want it to be a *snug harbour for tired sailors.*"

So the will, July 10, 1801, reads that Robert Richard Randall's property is left to found: "An Asylum or Marine Hospital, to be called 'The Sailors' Snug Harbour,' for the purpose of maintaining aged, decrepit, worn-out sailors."

One of the witnesses, by the bye, was Henry Brevoort.

The present bust of Randall which stands in the Asylum is, of course, quite apocryphal as to likeness. No one knows what he looked like, but out of such odds and ends of information as the knee-buckles and so on, mentioned in the will, the artistic imagination of St. Gaudens evolved a veritable beau of a mariner, with knee-buckles positively resplendent and an Admiral's wig. And, though it may not be a good likeness, it is an agreeable enough ideal, and I think everyone approves of it.

Robert Richard Randall is buried down there now and on his monument is a simple and rather impressive inscription commemorating this charity which - so it puts it - was "conceived in a spirit of enlarged Benevolence."

Shortly afterwards he died, but his will, in spite of the inevitable wrangling and litigation of disgusted relations, lived on, and the Snug Harbour for Tired Sailors is an accomplished fact. Randall had meant it to be built on his property there - a good "seeded-to-grass" farm land, - and thought that the grain and vegetables for the sailor inmates of this Snug Harbour on land could be grown on the premises. But the trustees decided to build the institution on Staten Island. The New York Washington Square property, however, is still called the Sailors' Snug Harbour Estate, and through its tremendous increase in value the actual asylum was benefited incalculably. At the time of Captain Randall's death, the New York estate brought in about $4,000 a year. Today it is about $400,000, - and every cent goes to that real Snug Harbour for Tired Sailors out near the blue waters of Staten Island. So the "honest privateering" fortune has made at least one impossible seeming dream come true.

As time went on this section - the Sailors' Snug Harbour Estate and the Brevoort property - was destined to become New York's most fashionable quarter. Its history is the history of American society, no less, and one can have no difficulty in visualising an era in which a certain naive ceremony combined in piquant fashion with the sturdy solidity of the young and vigorous country. In the correspondence of Henry Brevoort and Washington Irving and others one gets delightful little pictures - vignettes, as it were - of social life of that day. Mr. Emmet writes begging for some snuff "no matter how old. It may be stale and flat but cannot be unprofitable!" Brevoort asks a friend to dine "On Thursday next at half-past four o'clock." He paints us a quaint sketch of "a little, round old gentleman, returning heel taps into decanters," at a soiree, adding: "His heart smote him at beholding the waste & riot of his dear adopted." We read of tea drinkings and coaches and his father's famous blunderbuss or "long gun" which he is presenting to Irving. And there are other chroniclers of the times. Lossing, the historian, quotes an anonymous friend as follows:

> "We thought there was a goodly display of wealth and diamonds in those days, but, God bless my soul, when I hear of the millions amassed by the Vanderbilts, Goulds, Millses, Villards and others of that sort, I realise what a poor little doughnut of a place New York was at that early period!"

He goes on to speak of dinner at three - a formal dinner party at four. The first private carriage was almost mobbed on Broadway. Mrs. Jacob Little had "a very showy carriage lined with rose colour and a darky coachman in blue livery."

Mr. and Mrs. Henry Brevoort's house stood on the corner of Fifth Avenue and Ninth Street - it is now occupied by the Charles de Rhams. And it chanced to be the scene of a certain very pretty little romance which can scarcely be passed over here.

New York, as a matter of course, copied her fashionable standards from older lands. While Manhattan society was by no means a supine and merely imitative affair, the country was too new not to cling a bit to English and French formalities. The great ladies of the day made something of a point of their "imported amusements" as having a specific claim on fashionable favour. So it came about that the fascinating innovation of the masked ball struck the fancy of fashionable New York. There was something very daring about the notion; it smacked of Latin skies and manners and suggested possibilities of romance both licensed and not which charmed the ladies, even as it abashed them. There were those who found it a project scarcely in good taste; it is said indeed that there was no end of a flutter concerning it. But be that as it

Anna Alice Chapin

may, the masked ball was given, - the first that New York had ever known, and, it may be mentioned, the very last it was to know for many a long, discreet year!

Haswell says that in this year there was a "fancy" ball given by Mr. and Mrs. Henry Brevoort and that the date was February 24th. It certainly was the same one, but he adds that it was generally pronounced "most successful." This one may doubt, since the results made masked balls so severely thought of that there was, a bit later, a fine of $1,000 imposed on anyone who should give one, - one-half to be deducted if you told on yourself!

Nevertheless, George S. Hellman says that Mrs. Brevoort's ball, February 24, 1840, - was "the most splendid social affair of the first half of the nineteenth century in New York."

There was great preparation for it, and practically all "society" was asked - and nothing and nobody else. It was incidentally the occasion of the first "society reporting." Attree, of the New York *Herald*, was an invited guest and went in costume - quite an innovation for conservative old Manhattan.

Lossing tells us: "At the close of this decade the features of New York society presented conspicuous transformations. Many exotic customs prevailed, both public and private, and the expensive pleasures of the Eastern Hemisphere had been transplanted and taken firm root. Among other imported amusements was the masked ball, the first of which occurred in the city of New York in 1840, and produced a profound sensation, not only *per se*, but because of an attending circumstance which stirred 'society' to its foundation."

The British Consul in New York at that time was Anthony Barclay, - he lived at College Place, - who was destined later to fall into evil repute, by raising recruits here during the Crimean trouble. He had a daughter, Matilda, who was remarkably lovely and - if we may believe reports - a very great belle in American society. She had a number of "suitors," as they were gracefully called in those days, and among them was one Burgwyne, from South Carolina - very young, and, we may take it, rather poor.

Lossing says: "There was also in attendance a gay, young South Carolinian named Burgwyne."

The Consul and Mrs. Barclay disapproved of him strongly. But Matilda who was beautiful, warm-blooded and wayward did not. She loved Burgwyne with a reciprocal ardour, and when the masked ball at the Brevoorts' came on the tapis it seemed as though the Goddess of Romance had absolutely stretched out her hands to these two reckless, but adorable lovers.

They had a favourite poem - most lovers have favourite poems; - theirs was "Lalla Rookh."

There may be diverse opinions as to Thomas Moore's greatness, but there can scarcely be two as to his lyric gift. He could write charming love-songs, simple and yet full of colour, and, given the Oriental theme, it is no wonder that youths and maidens of his day sighed and smiled over "Lalla Rookh" as over nothing that had yet been written for them. It is a delightful tale, half-prose and half-poetry, written entirely and whole-heartedly for lovers, and Burgwyne and Matilda found it easy to put themselves in the places of the romantic characters in the drama - Lalla Rookh, the incomparably beautiful Eastern Princess and Feramorz, the young Prince in disguise, "graceful as that idol of women, Crishna."

They secretly agreed to go to the masked ball at the Brevoorts' as their romantic favourites and prototypes. The detailed descriptions in the book gave them sufficient inspiration. She wore floating gauzes, bracelets, "a small coronet of jewels" and "a rose-coloured, bridal veil." His dress was "simple, yet not without marks of costliness," with a "high Tartarian cap.... Here and there, too, over his vest, which was confined by a flowered girdle of Kaskan, hung strings of fine pearls, disposed with an air of studied negligence."

So they met at the ball and danced together, and I suppose he quoted:

> *"Fly to the desert, fly with me,*
> *Our Arab tents are rude for thee;*
> *But, oh! the choice what heart can doubt,*
> *Of tents with love, or thrones without?"*

Obviously she chose the tents with love, for as the clock struck four they slipped away together and were married!

As Lossing puts it:

> *"They left the festive scene together at four o'clock in the morning, and were married before breakfast."*

They did not change their costumes, dear things! They wanted the romantic trappings for their love poem - a love poem which was to them more enchanting - more miraculous - than that of Lalla Rookh and the King of Bucharia. I hope they lived happily ever after, like the brave, young romanticists they were!

In 1835 a hotel was opened on the corner of Eighth Street and Fifth Avenue, and it was appropriately named for the illustrious family over the way. The Brevoort House is certainly as historic a pile, socially speaking, as lower New York has to offer. Arthur Bartlett Maurice says of it:

> *"In the old-time novels of New York life visiting Englishmen invariably stopped at the Brevoort."*

Of this hotel more anon, since it has recently become knit into the fabric of the modern Village.

But a scant two blocks away from the Brevoort stands another hostelry which is indissolubly a part of New York's growth -

especially the growth of her Artist's Colony. It is the Lafayette, or as many of its habitues still love to call it - "The Old Martin." This, the first and most famous French restaurant of New York, needs a special word or two. It must be considered alone, and not in the company of lesser and more modern eating places.

John Reed says that the "Old Martin" was the real link between the old Village and the new, since it was the cradle of artistic life in New York. Bohemians, he declared, first foregathered there *as* Bohemians, and the beginnings of what has become America's Latin Quarter and Soho there first saw the light of day - or rather the lights of midnight.

Jean Baptiste Martin who had been running a hotel in Panama during the first excavations there - made by the French, as you may or may not remember - came to New York in 1883. He had been here the year before for a time and had decided the city needed a French hotel. He arrived on the 25th of June, and on the 26th he bought the hotel! He chose a house on University Place - No. 17 - a little *pension* kept by one Eugene Larru, and from time to time bought the adjoining houses and built extensions until he had made it the building we see today. He called it the Hotel de Panama.

But it was not as the Hotel de Panama that it won its unique place in the hearts of New Yorkers. "In 1886," Mr. Martin says, "I decided to change the name of my place. 'Panama' gave people a bad impression. They associated it with fever and Spaniards, and neither were popular! So it became the Hotel Martin. Then, when I started another restaurant at Twenty-sixth Street, the 'Old Martin' became the Lafayette."

The artists and writers came to the Hotel Martin to invite their respective Muses inspired by Mr. Martin's excellent food and drink. From the bachelors' quarters on the nearby square - the Benedick and other studio houses - shabby, ambitious young men came in droves. Mr. Martin remembers "Bob" Chambers, and some young newspaper men from the *World* - Goddard,

Manson and others. From uptown the great foreigners came down - some of them stayed there, indeed. In 1889, approximately, it started its biggest boom, and it went on steadily. Ask either Mr. Martin or its present proprietor, Mr. Raymond Orteig, and he will tell you, and truthfully, that it has never flagged, that "boom." The place is as popular as ever, because, in a changing world, a changing era and a signally changing town, it - does not change.

It was to the Hotel Martin that the famous singers came - Jean and Edouard de Reszke and Pol Plancon and Melba; the French statesman, Jules Cambon, used to come, and Maurice Grau - then the manager of the Metropolitan - and Chartran, the celebrated painter, and the great Ysaye and Bartholdi. And Paulus - Koster and Bial's first French importation - to say nothing of Anna Held and Sandow!

A motley company enough, to be sure, and certainly one worthy to form the nucleus of New York's Bohemia.

Says Mr. Martin: "The most interesting thing that ever happened in the 'Old Martin'? I can tell you that quite easily. It was the blizzard of 1888, when we were snowed in. The horse cars ran on University Place then, the line terminating at Barclay Street. I have a picture of one car almost snowed under, for the snow was fully six feet deep. It was a Saturday night and very crowded. When it became time for the people to go home they could not go. So they had to stay, and they stayed three days. They slept on billiard tables, on the floor or where they could. We did our best, but it was a big crowd. Interesting? It was most interesting indeed to me, for I could get no milk. I could supply them with all the wine they wanted, but no milk! And they demanded milk for their coffee. Oh, that blizzard!"

Mr. Martin, in remembering interesting episodes, forgot that trifling incident - the Spanish-American War, in 1898. Whether because of his early connections with Panama (there were countless Spaniards and Mexicans who patronised the hotel at that time) or whether because of a national and political misunderstanding, he was justifiably and seriously concerned as to the feeling of New York for the Hotel Martin. Many good and wise persons expected France to side with Spain, and many others watched curiously to see what Frenchmen in New York would do.

Mr. Martin left them but a short time for speculation. Today, with our streets aflutter with Allied colours, perhaps we fail to appreciate an individual demonstration such as this - but at that time there were few banners flying, and Mr. Martin led the patriotic movement with an American flag in every one of the fifty windows of the Hotel Martin and a French flag to top off the whole display! Perhaps it was the first suggestion, in street decoration, of what has recently proved to be so strong a bond between this nation and France.

If any of you who read have even begun to peer into Bohemian New York you have undoubtedly visited the Lafayette as it is today. And, if you have, you have undoubtedly seen or perhaps even played the "Lafayette Game." It is a weird little game that is played for drinks, and requires quite a bit of skill. It is well known to all frequenters; the only odd thing is that it is not better known.

"Americans are funny!" laughs Raymond Orteig. "When I go abroad and see something which is new and different from what has been before, my instinct is to get hold of it and bring it back. If I can I bring it back in actual bulk; if I were a writer I would bring it back in another way. But through these years, while everyone has played our absurd little game, no one has ever suggested writing about it - until tonight!"

Its name? It is *Culbuto*. That is French, - practically applied, - for failure! It is, you see, an effort to keep the little balls from falling into the wrong holes. As it so often results in failure *Culbuto* is an ideal game to play for drinks! Someone has to pay all the time! It is an unequal contest between the individual and the law of gravity!

Anna Alice Chapin

But we must not linger too long at the Lafayette, alluring though it may be. All Greenwich is beckoning to us, a few blocks away. We have a new world to explore - the world below Fourteenth Street.

Fourteenth Street is the boundary line which marks the Greenwich Village's utmost city limits, as it marked those of our great-grandfathers. Like a wall it stands across the town separating the new from the old uncompromisingly. Miss Euphemia Olcott, who has been quoted here before, describes the evolution of Fourteenth Street in the following interesting way:

> "Fourteenth Street between Fifth and Sixth Avenues I have seen with three sets of buildings - first shanties near Sixth Avenue from the rear of which it was rumoured a bogy would be likely to pursue and kidnap us.... These shanties were followed by fine, brownstone residences.... Some of these, however, I think came when there had ceased to be a *village*. Later on came business into Fourteenth Street...."

And today those never-to-be-sufficiently-pitied folk who live in the Fifties and Sixties and Seventies think of Fourteenth Street as downtown!

# CHAPTER VII

## RESTAURANTS, AND THE MAGIC DOOR

I

What scenes in fiction cling more persistently in the memory than those that deal with the satisfying of man's appetite? Who ever heard of a dyspeptic hero? Are not your favourites    beyond the Magic Door all good trenchermen?

- ARTHUR BARTLETT MAURICE.

It was O. Henry, I believe, who spoke of restaurants as "literary landmarks." They are really much more than that - they are signposts, psychical rather than physical, which show the trend of the times - or of the neighbourhood. I suppose nothing in Greenwich Village could be more significantly illuminating than its eating places. There are, of course, many sorts. The Village is neither so unique nor so uniform as to have only one sort of popular board. But in all the typical Greenwich restaurants you will find the same elusive something, the spirit of the picturesque, the untrammelled, the quaint and charming - in short, the *different*!

The Village is not only a locality, you understand, it is a point of view. It reaches out imperiously and fastens on what it will. The Brevoort basement - after ten o'clock at night - is the

Village. So is the Lafayette on occasion. During the day they are delightful French hostelries catering to all the world who like heavenly things to eat and the right atmosphere in which to eat them. But as the magic hour strikes, presto! - they suffer a sea change and become the quintessence of the Spirit of the Village!

It is 10.20 P.M. at the Brevoort in the restaurant upstairs. All the world and his wife - or his sweetheart - are fully represented. Most of the uptowners - the regulation clientele - are going away, having finished gorging themselves on delectable things; some few of them are lingering, lazily curious; a certain small number are still coming in, moved by that restless Manhattanic spirit that hates to go home in the dark.

Among these is a discontented, well-dressed couple, seen half an hour before completing their dinner a block away at the Lafayette. The head waiter at that restaurant explained them nonchalantly, not to say casually:

"It is the gentleman who married his manicurist. Regard, then - one perceives they are not happy - eh? It is understood that she beats him."

Yonder is a moving-picture star, quite alone, eating a great deal, and looking blissfully content. There is a man who has won a fortune in war-brides - the one at the next table did it with carpets. There is a great lady - a very great lady indeed - who, at this season, *should* be out of town.

Swiftly moving, deft-handed waiters, the faint perfume of delicate food, the sparkle of light upon rare wine, the complex murmur of a well-filled dining-room. It is so far not strikingly different, in the impression it gives, from uptown restaurants.

But the hands of the clock are pointing to the half-hour after ten.

Hasten, then, to the downstairs cafe, - the two rooms, sunk below the level of Fifth Avenue, yet cool and airy. If you hurry you will be just in time to see the Village come in. For this is their really favourite haunt - their Mecca when their pockets will stand it - the Village Restaurant de Luxe!

Upstairs are exquisite frocks and impeccable evening clothes; good jewels and, incidentally, a good many tired faces - from uptown. Down here it is different. The crowd is younger, poorer, more strikingly bizarre - immeasurably more interesting. Everyone here does something, or thinks he does - which is just as good; - or pretends to - which is next best. There is a startling number of girls. Girls in smocks of "artistic" shades - bilious yellow-green, or magenta-tending violet; girls with hair that, red, black or blonde, is usually either arranged in a wildly natural bird's-nest mass, or boldly clubbed after the fashion of Joan of Arc and Mrs. Vernon Castle; girls with tense little faces, slender arms and an astonishing capacity as to cigarettes. And men who, for the most part, are too busy with their ideals to cut their hair; men whose collars may be low and rolling, or high and bound with black silk stocks after the style of another day; men who are, variously, affectedly natural or naturally affected, but who are nearly all of them picturesque, and, in spite of their poses, quite in earnest, after their queer fashion. They are all prophets and seers down here; they wear their bizarre hair-cuts and unusual clothes with a certain innocently flaunting air which rather disarms you. Their poses are not merely poses; they are their almost childlike way of showing the prosaic outer world how different they are!

Here they all flock - whenever they have the price. That may be a bit beyond them sometimes, but usually there is someone in the crowd who is "flush," and that means who will pay. For the Villagers are not parsimonious; they stand in no danger of ever making themselves rich and thus acquiring place in the accursed class called the Philistines!

It is beyond question that the French have a genius for

hospitality. It must be rooted in their beautiful, national tact, that gracious impulse combining chivalry to women, friendliness to men and courtesy to all which is so characteristic of "the world's sweetheart" France. I have never seen a French restaurant where the most casual visitor was not made personally and charmingly welcome, and I have never seen such typically French restaurants as the Lafayette and the Brevoort. And the Villagers feel it too. From the shabbiest socialist to the most flagrantly painted little artist's model, they drift in thankfully to that atmosphere of gaiety and sympathy and thoughtful kindliness which is, after all, just - the air of France.

Next let us take a restaurant of quite another type, not far from the Brevoort - all the Village eating places are close together - walk across the square, a block further, and you are there.

It is not many years since Bohemia ate chiefly in the side streets, at restaurants such as Enrico's, Baroni's - there are a dozen such places. They still exist, but the Village is dropping away from them. They are very good and very cheap, and the tourist - that is, the uptowner - thinks he is seeing Bohemia when he eats in them, but not many of them remain at all characteristic. Bertolotti's is something of an exception. It is a restaurant of the old style, a survival of the days when all Bohemian restaurants were Italian. La Signora says they have been there, just there on Third Street, for twenty years. If you are a newcomer you will probably eat in the upstairs room, in cool and rather remote grandeur, and the pretty daughter with the wondrous black eyes will serve you the more elaborate of the most extraordinarily named dishes on the menu. But if, by long experience, you know what is pleasant and comfortable you will take a place in the basement cafe. At the clean, bare table, in the shadow of the big, bright, many-bottled bar, you will eat your *Risotta alla Milanese*, your *coteletti di Vitelle*, your *asparagi* - it's probably the only place in the city where they serve asparagus with grated cheese - finally your *zambaione*, - a heavenly sort of hot "flip," very foamy and seductive and strongly flavoured with Marsarla wine.

If you stand well with the house you may have the honour to be escorted by the Signora herself - handsome, dignified, genial, with a veritable coronal of splendid grey hair - to watch the eternal bowling in the alley back of the restaurant. I have watched them fascinated for long periods and I have never learned what it is they are trying to do with those big "bowling balls." They have no ninepins, so they are not trying to make a ten-strike. Apparently, it is a game however, for now and then a shout of triumph proclaims that someone has won. He orders the drinks and they go at it again.

"But, what *is* it?" I asked the Signora.

"Eh - oh - just a *Giocho di Bocca*," she returned vaguely, "a game of bowls - how should I know?"

Beyond the bowling alley is a long, narrow yard with bushes. It would make quite a charming summer garden with little tables for after-dinner coffee. But the Signora says that the *Chiesa*, there at the back of it, objects. The *Chiesa*, I think, is the Judson Memorial Church on Washington Square. Just why they don't want the Signora to have tables in her own back yard is not clear. She, being a Latin, shrugs her shoulders and makes no comment. Standing in the darkness, there is a real freshness in the air; there is also a delicious, gurgling sound, the music of summer streams.

"How lovely!" you whisper. "What a delightful, rippling sound."

"Yet, it is the ice plant of the big hotel," says La Signora sweetly.

There is, at Bertolotti's one of the queerest little old figures in all that part of the world, the bent and aged Italian known universally as *Castagna* (Chestnuts), because of the interminable anecdotes he tells over and over again. No one knows his real name, not even the Signor or the Signora. Yet he has worked for them for years. He wants no wages - only a living and a home. In the aforementioned back yard he has built himself a little house about the size of a dog kennel. It is a real house, and like nothing so much as the historic residence of the Three Bears. It has a window, eaves, weather-strips and a clothesline, for he does his own washing. He trots off there very happily when his light work is done, and, when his door is closed, opens it for no one. That scrap of a building is *Castagna's* castle. One evening I went to call on him, but he had put out his light. In the gleam that came from the bowling alley behind me, something showed softly red and green and white against the wooden door. I put out my hand and touched that world-famous cross. It was about six inches long, and only of paper, but it was the flag of Italy, and it kept watch outside the *Casa Castagna.* I am certain that he would not sleep well without it.

Probably the most famous Bohemian restaurant in the quarter is the Black Cat. It is not really more typical than the others, - indeed it is rather less so, - but it is extremely striking, and most conspicuous. There is, in the minds of the hypercritical, the sneaking suspicion that the Black Cat is almost too good to be true; it is too obviously and theatrically lurid with the glow of Montmartre; it is Bohemianism just a shade too much conventionalised. Just the same, it is fascinating. From the moment you pass the outer, polite portals and intermediate anterooms and enter the big, smoke-filled, deafening room at the back, you are enormously interested, excellently entertained. The noise is the thing that impresses you first. In most Village resorts you find quiet the order of the day - or rather night. Even "Polly's," crowded as it is, is not noisy. In the Brevoort there is a steady, low rumble of talk, but not actual noise. At the Black Cat it is one continual and all-pervading roar - a joyous roar, too; these people are having a simply gorgeous time and don't care who knows it. It is a wonder that the high-set rafters do not fall - that the lofty, whitewashed walls of brick do not tremble, and that the little black cats set in a rigid conventional design around the whole room do not come to life in horror, and fly spitting up the short stairway and out of the door!

When you go to the Black Cat you would better check what prejudices you have as to what is formal and fitting, and leave them with your coat at the entrance. Not that it is disreputable - Luigi would pale with the shock of such a thought! It is just - Bohemian! Everyone does exactly what he wishes to do. Sometimes, one person's wishes conflict with someone else's, and then there is a fight, and the police are called, and the rest of the patrons have a beautiful time watching a perfectly good and unexpected free show! As a rule, however, this determination on the part of each one to do what he wants to has no violent results. An incident will show something of the entire liberty allowed in the Black Cat. A man came in with two girls, and, seeing a jolly stag party at another table, decided to join them. He promptly did so, with, as far as could be seen, no word of excuse to his feminine companions. In a moment two young men strolled up to their table and sat down.

"Your friend asked us to come over here and take his place," explained one nonchalantly. "You don't object, ladies?"

The girls received them amiably. Apparently no one thought of such a formality as names or introductions. The original host stayed away for the rest of the evening, but the four new acquaintances seemed to get along quite satisfactorily without him.

A young married woman from uptown came in with her husband and two other men. A good-looking lad, much flushed and a little unsteady, stopped by her chair.

"Say, k-kid," he exclaimed, with a disarming chuckle, "you're the prettiest girl here - and you come here with three p-protectors! Say, it's a shame!"

He lurched cheerfully upon his way and even the slightly conservative husband found a grudging smile wrung out of him.

There is a pianist at the Black Cat - a real pianist, not just a person who plays the piano. She is a striking figure in a quaint, tunic-like dress, greying hair and a keen face, and a personal friend of half the frequenters. She has an uncanny instinct for the psychology of the moment. She knows just when "Columbia" will be the proper thing to play, and when the crowd demands the newest rag-time. She will feel an atmospheric change as unswervingly as any barometer, and switch in a moment from "Good-bye Girls, Good-bye" to the love duet from Faust. She can play Chopin just as well as she can play Sousa, and she will tactfully strike up "It's Always Fair Weather" when she sees a crowd of young fellows sit down at a table; "There'll Be a Hot Time in the Old Town Tonight" to welcome a lad in khaki; and the very latest fox trot for the party of girls and young men from uptown, who look as though they were dying to dance. She plays the "Marseillaise" for Frenchmen, and "Dixie" for visiting Southerners, and "Mississippi" for the frequenters of Manhattan vaudeville shows. And, then, at the right moment, her skilled fingers will drift suddenly into something different, some exquisite, inspired melody - the soul-child of some high immortal - and under the spell the noisy crowd grows still for a moment. For even at the Black Cat they have not forgotten how to dream.

Probably the Black Cat inspired many other Village restaurants - the Purple Pup for instance.

The Purple Pup is a queer little place. It is in a most exclusive and aristocratic part of the Square - in the basement of one of the really handsome houses, in fact. It is, so far as is visible to the naked eye, quite well conducted, yet there is something mysterious about it. Doubtless this is deliberately stage-managed and capitalised, but it is effectively done. It is an unexpected sort of place. One evening you go there and find it in full blast; the piano tinkling, many cramped couples dancing in the two tiny rooms, and every table covered with tea cups or lemonade glasses. Another night you may arrive at exactly the same time and there will be only candlelight and a few groups, talking in low tones.

Here, as in all parts of the Village, the man in the rolling collar, and the girl in the smock, will be markedly in evidence. Yes; they really do look like that. Lots of the girls have their hair cut short too.

And "Polly's"!

In many minds, "Polly's" and the Village mean one and the same thing. Certainly no one could intelligently write about the one without due and logical tribute to the other. Polly Holliday's restaurant (The Greenwich Village Inn is its formal name in the telephone book) is not incidental, but institutional. It is fixed, representative and sacred, like Police Headquarters, Trinity Church and the Stock Exchange. It is indispensable and independent. The Village could not get along without it, but the Village no longer talks about it nor advertises it. It is, in fact, so obviously a vital part of Greenwich that often enough a Greenwicher, asked to point out hostelries of peculiar interest, will forget to mention it.

"How about 'Polly's'?" you remind him.

"Oh - but 'Polly's'!" he protests wonderingly. "Why, it wouldn't be the Village at all without 'Polly's.' It - why, of course, I never thought anyone had to be told about *'Polly's'*!"

His attitude will be as disconcerted as though you asked him whether he was in the habit of using air to breathe, - or was accustomed to going to bed to sleep.

Polly Holliday used to have her restaurant under the Liberal Club - where the Dutch Oven is now, - but now she has her own good-sized place on Fourth Street, and it remains, through fluctuations and fads, the most thoroughly and consistently popular Village eating place extant. It is, outwardly, not original nor superlatively striking in any way. It is a clean, bare place with paper napkins and such waits between courses as are unquestionably conducive to the encouragement of philosophic, idealistic, anarchistic and aesthetic debates. But the food is excellent, when you get it, and the atmosphere both friendly and - let us admit frankly - inspiring. The people are interesting; they discuss interesting things. You are comfortable, and you are exhilarated. You see, quickly enough, why the Village could not possibly get along without its inn; why "Polly's" is so essential a part of its life that half the time it overlooks it. Outsiders always know about "Polly's." But the Villager?

"'Polly's'? But *of course* 'Polly's.'"

There it is. *Of course* "Polly's." "Polly's" is Greenwich Village in little; it is, in a fashion, cosmic and symbolic.

Under the Liberal Club, where "Polly's" used to be located, the "Dutch Oven," with its capacious fireplace and wholesome meals, now holds sway. The prices are reasonable, the food substantial and the atmosphere comfortable, so it is a real haven of good cheer to improvident Villagers.

The Village Kitchen on Greenwich Avenue is another place of the same sort. And Gallup's - almost the first of these "breakfast and lunch" shops - is another. They are not unlike a Childs restaurant, but with the rarefied Village air added. You eat real food in clean surroundings, as you do in Childs', but you do it to an accompaniment that is better than music - a sort of life-song, rather stirring and quite touching in its way - the Song of the Village. How can people be both reckless and deeply earnest? But the Villagers are both.

One of the oddest sights on earth is a typical "Breakfast" at "Polly's," the "Kitchen" or the "Dutch Oven," after one of the masked balls for which the Village has recently acquired such a passion. After you have been up all night in some of these mad masquerades - of which more anon - you may not, by Village convention, go home to bed. You must go to breakfast with the rest of the Villagers. And you must be prepared to face the cold, grey dawn of "the morning after" while still in your war paint and draggled finery. It is an awful ordeal. But "it's being done in the Village"!

Quite recently a new sort of eating place has sprung up in Greenwich Village - of so original and novel a character that we must investigate it in at least a few of its manifestations. Speaking for myself, I had never believed that such places could exist within sound of the "L" and a stone's throw from drug stores and offices.

But see what you think of them.

II

"I can't believe *that*!" said Alice.

"Can't you?" the Queen said in a pitying tone. "Try again: draw a long breath and shut your eyes."

Alice laughed. "There's no use trying," she said. "One *can't* believe impossible things.'

"I daresay you haven't had much practice," said the Queen. "When I was your age, I always did it for half-an-hour a day. Why, sometimes I've believed as many as six impossible things before breakfast."

- "THROUGH THE LOOKING GLASS."

"But it can't be this!" I said. "You've made a mistake in the number!"

"It is this," declared my guide and companion. "This is where Nanni Bailey has her tea shop."

"But this is - is - isn't anything!"

Indeed the number to which my friend pointed seemed to indicate the entrance to a sort of warehouse, if it indicated anything at all. On peering through the dim and gloomy doorway, it appeared instead to be a particularly desolate-looking cellar. There were old barrels and boxes about, an expanse of general dusty mystery and, in the dingy distance, a flight of ladder-like steps leading upwards to a faint light.

"It's one of Dickens' impossible stage sets come true!" I exclaimed. "It looks as though it might be a burglars' den or somebody's back yard, but anyway, it isn't a restaurant!"

"It is too!" came back at me triumphantly. "Look at that sign!" By the faint rays of a street light on nearby Sixth Avenue, I saw the shabby little wooden sign, "The Samovar." This extraordinary place was a restaurant after all!

We entered warily, having a vague expectation of pickpockets or rats, and climbed that ladder - I mean staircase - to what was purely and simply a loft.

But such a loft! Such a quaint, delicious, simple, picturesque apotheosis of a loft! A loft with the rough bricks whitewashed and the heavy rafters painted red; a loft with big, plain tables and a bare floor and an only slightly partitioned-off kitchenette where the hungry could descry piles of sandwiches and many coffee cups. And there in the middle of the loft was the Samovar itself, a really splendid affair, and one actually not for decorative purposes only, but for use. I had always thought samovars were for the ornamentation either of houses or foreign-atmosphere novels. But you could use this thing. I saw people go and get glasses-full of tea out of it.

Under the smoke-dimmed lights were curious, eager, interesting faces: a pale little person with red hair I recognised instantly as an actress whom I had just seen at the Provincetown Players - a Village Theatrical Company - in a tense and terribly tragic role. Beyond her was a white-haired man with keen eyes - a distinguished writer and socialist. A shabby poet announced to the sympathetic that he had sold something after two years of work. Immediately they set about making a real fiesta of the unusual occasion. Miss Bailey, a small, round, efficient person with nice eyes and good manners, moved about among her guests, all of whom she seemed to know. The best cheese sandwiches in New York went round. A girl in a vampire costume of grey - hooded and with long trailing sleeves - got up from her solitary place in the corner. She seemed to be wearing, beneath the theatrical garment, a kimono and bedroom slippers. Obviously she had simply drifted in for andwiches before going to bed. She vanished down the ladder.

An hour later, we, too, climbed down the ladderish stairs, my companion and I, and as we came out into the fresh quiet of Fourth Street at midnight, I had a really odd sensation. I felt as though I had been reading a fascinating and unusual book, and had - suddenly closed it for the night.

This was one of the first of the real Village eating places which I ever knew. Perhaps that is why it comes first to my memory as I write. I do not know that it is more representative or more interesting than others. But it was worth going back to.

Yet, after all, it isn't the food and drink, nor yet the unusual surroundings, that bring you back to these places. It's the - well, one has to use, once in a while, the hard-worked and generally inappropriate word "atmosphere." Like "temperament" and "individuality" and the rest of the writer-folk's old reliables, "atmosphere" is too often only a makeshift, a lazy way of expressing something you won't take the trouble to define more expressively. Dick says in "The Light That Failed" that an old device for an unskilful artist is to stick a superfluous bunch of flowers somewhere in a picture where it will cover up bad drawing. I'm afraid writers are apt to use stock phrases in the same meretricious fashion.

But this is a fact just the same. Nearly all the Greenwich Village places really have atmosphere. You can be cynical about it, or frown at it, or do anything you like about it, but it's there, and it's the real thing. It's an absolute essence and ether which you feel intensely and breathe necessarily, but which no one can put quite definitely into the concrete form of words. I have heard of liquid or solidified air, but that's a scientific experiment, and who wants to try scientific experiments on the Village which we all love?

"But such an amount of play-acting and pose!" I hear someone complain, referring to the Village with contemptuous irritation. "They pretend to be seeking after truth and liberty of thought, and that sort of thing, and yet they are steeped in artificiality."

Yes, to a certain extent that is true - true of a portion of the Village, at any rate, and a certain percentage of the Villagers. But even if it is true, it is the sort of truth that needs only a bit of understanding to make us tender and tolerant instead of scornful and hard. My dear lady, you who complained of the "play-acting," and you other who, agreeing with her, see in the whimsies and pretenses in Our Village only a spectacle of cheap affectation and artifice, have you lived so long and yet do not know that the play-acting instinct is one of the most universal of all instincts - the very first developed, and the very last, I truly believe, to die in our faded bodies? From the moment when we try to play ball with sunbeams through those intermediate years wherein we imagine ourselves everything on earth that we are not, down to those last days of all, when we live, all furtive and unsuspected, a secret life of the spirit - either a life of remembrance or a life of imagination visualising what we have wanted and have missed, - what do we do but pretend, - make believe, - pose, if you will? When we are little we pretend to be knights and ladies, pirates and fairy princesses, soldiers and Red Cross nurses, and sailors and hunters and explorers. We people the window boxes with elves and pixies and the dark corners with Red Indians and bears. The commonplace world about us is not truly commonplace, since our fancy, still fresh from eternity, can transform three dusty shrubs into an enchanted forest, and an automobile into the most deliciously formidable of the Dragon Family. A bit later, our pretending is done more cautiously. We do not confess our shy flights of imagination: we take a prosaic outward pose, and try not to advertise the fact that our geese wear (to our eyes) swans' plumage, and that our individual roles are (to our own view) always those of heroes and heroines. No one of us but mentally sees himself or herself doing something which is as impracticable as cloud-riding. No one of us but dreams of the impossible and in a shamefaced, almost clandestine, fashion pictures it and lingers over it. All make-believe, you see, only we hate to admit it! The different thing about Greenwich is that there they do admit it, quite a number of them. They accept the pretending, play-acting spirit as a perfectly natural - no, as an inevitable - part of life, and,

Anna Alice Chapin

with a certain whimsical seriousness, not unlike that of real children, they provide for it. You know children can make believe, *know* that it is make believe, yet enjoy it all the more for that. So can the Villagers. Hence, places like - let us say, as an example - "The Pirate's Den."

It is a very real pirate's den, lighted only by candles. A coffin casts a shadow, and there is a regulation "Jolly Roger," a black flag ornamented with skull and crossbones. Grim? Surely, but even a healthy-minded child will play at gruesome and ghoulish games once in a while.

There is a Dead Man's Chest too, - and if you open it you will find a ladder leading down into mysterious depths unknown. If you are very adventurous you will climb down and bump your head against the cellar ceiling and inspect what is going to be a subterranean grotto as soon as it can be fitted up. You climb up again and sit in the dim, smoky little room and look about you. It is the most perfect pirate's den you can imagine. On the walls hang huge casks and kegs and wine bottles in their straw covers, - all the signs manual of past and future orgies. Yet the "Pirate's Den" is "dry" - straw-dry, brick-dry - as dry as the Sahara. If you want a "drink" the well-mannered "cut-throat" who serves you will give you a mighty mug of ginger ale or sarsaparilla. And if you are a real Villager and can still play at being a real pirate, you drink it without a smile, and solemnly consider it real red wine filched at the edge of the cutlass from captured merchantmen on the high seas. On the big, dark centre table is carefully drawn the map of "Treasure Island."

The pirate who serves you (incidentally he writes poetry and helps to edit a magazine among other things) apologises for the lack of a Stevensonian parrot.

"A chap we know is going to bring one back from the South Sea Islands," he declares seriously. "And we are going to teach it to say, 'Pieces of eight! Pieces of eight!'"

If, while you are at the "Pirate's Den" you care to climb a rickety, but enchanted staircase outside the old building (it's pre-Revolutionary, you know) you will come to the "Aladdin Shop" - where coffee and Oriental sweets are specialties. It is a riot of strange and beautiful colour - vivid and Eastern and utterly intoxicating. A very talented and picturesque Villager has painted every inch of it himself, including the mysterious-looking Arabian gentleman in brilliantly hued wood, who sits cross-legged luring you into the little place of magic. The wrought iron brackets on the wall are patches of vivid tints; the curtains at the windows are colour-dissonances, fascinating and bizarre. As usual there is candlelight. And, as usual, there is the same delicious spirit of seriously and whole-heartedly playing the game. While you are there you are in the East. If it isn't the East to you, you can go away - back to Philistia.

And speaking of candlelight. I went into the poets' favourite "Will o' the Wisp" tea shop once and found the gas-jet lighted! The young girl in charge jumped up, much embarrassed, and turned it out.

"I'm so sorry!" she apologised. "But I wanted to *see* just a moment, and lighted it!"

I peered at her face in the ghostly candlelight. It was entirely and unmistakably earnest.

Just the same, Mrs. Browning's warning that "colours seen by candlelight do not look the same by day" is not truly applicable to these Village shrines. Even under the searching beams of a slanting, summer afternoon sun, they are adorable. Go and see if you don't believe this.

Then take the "Mad Hatter's." The entrance alone is a monument to the make-believe capabilities of the Village. Scrawled on the stone wall beside the steps that lead down to the little basement tea room, is an inscription in chalk. It looks like anything but English. But if you held a looking-glass up to it you would find that it is "Down the Rabbit Hole" written backward! Now, if you know your "Alice" as well as you should, you will recall delightedly her dash after the White Rabbit which brought her to Wonderland, and, incidentally, to the Mad Tea Party.

You go in to the little room where Villagers are drinking tea, and the proprietress approaches to take your order. She is a good-looking young woman dressed in a bizarre red and blue effect, not unlike one of the Queens, but she prefers to be known as the "Dormouse" - not, however, that she shows the slightest tendency to fall asleep.

On the wall is scribbled, "'There's plenty of room,' said Alice."

The people around you seem only pleasantly mad, not dangerously so. There is a girl with an enchanting scrap of a monkey; there is a youth with a manuscript and a pile of cigarette butts. The great thing here once more is that they are taking their little play and their little stage with a heavenly seriousness, all of them. You expect somebody to produce a set of flamingos at any moment and start a game of croquet among the tiny tables.

Not all of the Greenwich restaurants have definite individual characters to maintain consistently. Sometimes it is just a general spirit of picturesqueness, of adventure, that they are trying to keep up. The "Mouse Trap," except for the trap hanging outside and a mouse scrawled in chalk on the wall of the entry, carries out no particular suggestion either of traps or mice. But take a look at the proprietress (Rita they call her), with her gorgeous Titian hair and delft-blue apron; at her son Sidney, fair, limp, slim, English-voiced, with a deft way of pouring after-dinner coffee, and hair the colour of corn. They are obviously play-acting and enjoying it.

Ask Rita her nationality. She will fix you with eyes utterly devoid of a twinkle and answer: "I? I am part Scotch terrier, and part Spanish mongrel, but *mostly* mermaid!"

Rita goes to the sideboard to cut someone a slice of good-looking pie. She overhears a reference to the "Candlestick," a little eating place chiefly remarkable for its vegetables and poetesses.

"If they eat nothing but vegetables no wonder they take to poetry," is her comment. But still she does not smile. If you giggle, as every child knows, you spoil the game. They laugh heartily enough and often enough down in the Village, but they never laugh at the Village itself, - not because they take it so reverentially, but because they know how to make believe altogether too well.

Let me whisper here that the most fascinating hour in the "Mouse Trap" is in the late afternoon, when no one is there, and the ebony hand-maiden in the big back kitchen is taking the fat, delicious-smelling cakes from the oven. Drop in some afternoon and sniff the fragrance that suggests your childhood and "sponge-cake day." You will feel that it is a trap no sane mouse would ever think of leaving! On a table beside you is a slate with, obviously, the day's specials:

"Spice cakes.
Chocolate cake.
Strawberry tarts with whipped cream."

And still as you peep through the door at the back you see more and still more goodies coming hot and fresh and enticing from the oven. White cakes, golden cakes, delicately browned pies, - if you are dieting by any chance you flee temptation and leave the "Mouse Trap" behind you.

It would be impossible to give even an approximately complete inventory of the representative places of the Village. I have had to content myself with some dozen or so examples, - recorded almost haphazard, for the most part, but as I believe, more or less typical, take them all in all, of the Village eating place in its varied and rather curious manifestations.

Then there is a charming shop presided over by a pretty girl with the inevitable smock and braided hair, where tea is served in order to entice you to buy carved and painted trifles.

And then there is, or was, the place kept by Polly's brother, which was heartlessly raided by the police, and much maligned, not to say libelled, by the newspapers.

And then there was and is the "Hell Hole." Its ancient distinction used to be that it was one of the first cheap Bohemian places where women could smoke, and that it was always open. When all the other resorts closed for the night you repaired to the "Hell Hole." As to the smoking, it has taken a good while for New York to allow its Bohemian women this privilege, though society leaders have enjoyed it for ages. We all know that though most fashionable hotels permitted their feminine guests to smoke, the Haymarket of dubious memory always tabooed the custom to the bitter end!

The "Hell Hole" has always stoutly approved of cigarettes, so all honour to it! And many a happy small-hours party has brought up there to top off the night in peace without having to keep an eye on the clock.

There is a little story told about one of these restaurants of which I have been writing - never mind which. A visiting Englishman on his way from his boat to his hotel dropped in at a certain place for a drink. He found the company congenial and drifted into a little game which further interested him. It was a perfectly straight game, and he was a perfectly good sport. He stayed there two weeks. No: I shall *not* state what the place was. But I think the story is true.

Personally, I don't blame the Englishman. Even shorn of the charm of a game of chance, there is many a place in Greenwich Village which might easily capture a susceptible temperament - not merely for weeks, but for years!

The last of the tea shops is the "Wigwam," in which, take note, it is the Indian game that is played. Its avowed aim is "Tea and Dancing," and it is exceedingly proud of its floor. It lives in the second story of what, for over fifty years, has been the old Sheridan Square Tavern, and its proprietors are the Mosses, - poet, editor and incidental "pirate" on one side of the house; and designer of enchanting "art clothes" on the other. Lew Kirby Parrish, no less, has made the decorations, and he told me that the walls were grey with Indian decorations, and the ceiling a "live colour." I discovered that that meant a vivid, happy orange.

The spirit of the play is always kept in the Village. Let us take the opening night of the "Wigwam" as a case in point.

The Indian note is supreme. It is not only the splendid line drawings of Indian chiefs, forming the panels of the room - those mysterious and impressive shades created by the imagination of Lew Parrish - it is the general mood. Only candles are burning, - big, fat candles, giving, in the aggregate, a magical radiance.

The victrola at the end of the room begins to play a curious Indian air with an uneven, fascinating, syncopated rhythm. A graceful girl in Indian dress glides in and places a single candle on the floor, squatting before it in a circle of dim, yellow light.

She lifts her dark head with its heavy band about the brows and shades her eyes with her hand. You see remote places, far, pale horizons, desert regions of sand. There are empty skies overhead, instead of the "live-colour" ceiling. With an agile movement, she rises and begins to dance about the candle, and you know that to her it is a little campfire; it is that to you, too, for the moment. Something like the west wind blows her fringed dress; there is a dream as old as life in her eyes.

Faster and faster she dances about the candle, until at last she sinks beside it and with a strange sure gesture - puts it out.

Silence and the dark. The prairie fades.... The little dark-wood tables with their flowers and candles begin to glow again; the next musical number is a popular one step!...

# CHAPTER VIII

## VILLAGERS

Although the serious affairs of life are met as conscientiously by the man or woman who has the real spirit of the Village, nevertheless each of them assuredly shows less of that sordidness and mad desire for money so prevalent throughout the land....

The real villager's life is better balanced. He produces written words of value, or material objects that offer utility and delight. *He sings his songs. He has a good time.* –

- From the INK POT (a Greenwich Village paper).

I quoted the above to a practical friend and he countered by quoting Dickens' delightful fraud, "Harold Skimpole":

"This is where the bird lives and sings! They pluck his feathers now and then, and clip his wings, but he sings, he sings!... Not an ambitious note, but still he sings!"

And my friend proceeded heartlessly: "'Skimpole' would have made a perfect Villager!"

It is hard to answer cold prose when your arguments are those of warm poetry. Not that prose has power to conquer poetry, but that the languages are so hopelessly dissimilar. They need

Anna Alice Chapin

an interpreter and the post is not a sinecure.

I want to try to throw a few dim sidelights on these Villagers whom I love and whom I know to be as alien to the average metropolitan consciousness and perception as though they were aboriginal representatives of interior and unexplored China. They are perhaps chiefly strange because of their ridiculous and lovely simplicity.

The artistic instinct, or impulse, is not particularly rare. Many persons have a real love for beautiful things, even a real aptitude for designing or reproducing them. The creative instinct is something vastly different. Creative artists, - great painters or sculptors, great illustrators, and wizards in pencil and pen and charcoal effects, - must be both born and made; and there are, the gods know, few enough of them, all told! Until comparatively recent times, everyone gifted with the blessing of an artistic sense turned it into a curse by trying to paint, draw or model, while the world yawned, laughed, turned away in disgust; and the real artists flung up their hands to heaven and cried: "What next?"

But lately, - in many places, but preeminently in Greenwich Village, - these folk who love art, but can't achieve great art expression, have evolved a new sort of art life. They are developing the embryo of what was the arts-and-crafts idea into a really fine, useful and satisfying art form. They have left mission furniture and Morris designs behind. They are making their own models, and making them well. They are turning their restless, beauty-loving energies into sound, constructive channels. The girl who otherwise might have painted atrocious pictures is, in the Village, decorating delightful-looking boxes and jars, or hammering metals into quaint, original shapes that embody her own fleeting fancies. The man who wanted to draw but could never get his perspective right is carving wood - a work where perspective is superfluous - and achieving pleasure for others, and comfort and a livelihood for himself, at one and the same time.

I know of nothing which is so typical or so significant in all the Village as this new urge toward good craftsmanship, elementary poetic design, - the fundamentals of a utilitarian, beautiful and pervading art life apart from clay or canvas.

The capitol of the Village shifts a bit from time to time, as befits so flexible, so fluid a community. Just at the present writing, it is at Sheridan Square that you will find it most colourfully and picturesquely represented. Tomorrow, no man may be able to say whence it has flitted.

You will find much golden sunshine in Sheridan Square - not the approved atmosphere of Bohemia, yet the real thing nevertheless. It is a broad, clean, brazen sort of sunshine - a sunshine that should say, "See me work! See me shine! See me show up the least last ugliness or smallness or humbleness, and glorify it to something Village-like and picturesque!"

When you leave the sunny square, you will enter the oddest little court in all New York; it has not to my knowledge any name, but it is the general address of enough tea shops and studios and Village haunts to stock an entire neighbourhood. The buildings are old - old, and, of course, of wood. These artist folk have metamorphosed the shabby and dilapidated structures into charming places.

Following the sign of deep blue with yellow letters which indicates that this is the place where the Hand-Painted Wooden Toys are made, you must climb in the sunshine up the outside staircase, which looks as though it had been put up for scaffolding purposes and then forgotten. Pausing on the rickety stairway and looking out beyond the crazy little court and over the drowsy Square, you will have a great deal of difficulty in believing that you left your cable car about a minute and a half before. Pass on up the stairs. You may nearly fall over the black-and-white feline which belongs to no one in any of the buildings, but which haunts them all like an unquiet ghost, and which is known by everyone as the Crazy Cat; so to the door of the studio-workshop where the toys are made.

And have you ever seen anything quite like that workshop?

A little light studio full of colour and the smell of paint. On one side blue-green boxes stacked on shelves; on the other finished sample toys not ready to be boxed. Shallow dishes of orange and emerald green and bright pink and primrose and black and vivid blue.

"Yes," says the girl who is working there - she is fair and wears a pale-green frock and a black work-apron, - "I do this part. Mr. Dickerman, the artist, makes the pictures or designs, then we have them turned out by the mill. See" - she shows queer shaped pieces of wood that suggest nothing to the casual observer - "Then the rest is done here!"

The room is full of all manner of curious and charming playthings. Here is a real pirate's chest for your treasures - the young workwoman is just painting the yellow nails on it - and here is a fierce-looking pirate with a cutlass for a bookshelf end; here is a futurist coat-hanger - a cubist-faced burglar with a jaw and the peremptory legend: "Give me your hat, scarf and coat!" Here is a neatly capped little waiting maid whose arms are constructed for flower holders; here are delightful watering-pots, exquisitely painted; wonderful cake covers, powder-boxes, blotters, brackets; - every single thing a little gem of clever design and individual workmanship. It is more fascinating than Toyland or Santa Claus' shop. These "rocking toys" are particularly fascinating: the dreadnought that careens at perilous angles, and the kicking mule which knocks its driver over as often as you like to make it. Shelves on shelves of these wonder-things complete, and a whole great table laden with them in half-finished forms. Some of the little wooden figures are set in a long rack to dry, for after the shellac has hardened each colour is put on and allowed to dry thoroughly before applying the next. The flesh-coloured enamel goes on first, then the other lighter shades, leaving the darker for the last, and the inevitable touches of black to finish off with.

"This way," says the girl in the black apron (which is really a smock), taking up a squat but adorable little wooden figure which is already coloured all over, but has a curiously unfinished aspect nevertheless. She fills a tiny brush with glittering, black enamel and begins to apply it in dots and lines. "This long dab is supposed to be his gun. These two little squares of black make his belt. One line for his trousers, - now he's done. He's for a blotter."

The little soldier has now taken on character and solidity as though by magic. He grins at us, very martial and smart indeed, as he is stood in the rack for the enamel to harden.

No one who has ever been to the workroom of one of those art shops will ever forget it. Personally I found it more enchanting than any regular studio I ever visited. There was quite real art there. Remember, those designs show no mean order of genius and imagination, and the more mechanical work is beautifully done and is constantly given a little individual, quaint twist which stamps the toys as personal works of art. And the whole picture, - I wish I could paint it! The low-ceilinged room, set high up above the little court; the sunshine and the golden square outside; the girl in the black smock and the huge table covered with pots and saucers and jars of every shape and size; and the vivid splashes of colour in the bright afternoon light - scarlet and violet and yellow and indigo and red-brown. And the wall full of strange and brilliant little figures grinning, scowling and staring down like so many goblins!

Just as you go out of the studio your eye can scarcely fail to fall upon one particular wooden hanger to be screwed on a door. If you know the "Rose and the Ring" by heart, as you should, it will give you quite a shock. It is the image of the Doorknocker into which the Fairy Blackstick changed the wicked porter Gruffanuff! It is indeed!

You know, if all these toys should come to life some moonlit night they would make quite a formidable array! Imagine the pirates and the kicking mules and the cubist burglars all running wild together! And there is something uncanny about them and their expressions that makes one suspect that such an event is more than half likely.

Even the advertisements for such a shop could not be commonplace. The artist in charge proclaims that: "Pirates are his specialty, and that he will gladly furnish estimates on anything from the services of a Pirate Crew to a Treasure Island or a Pirate Ship."

On Washington Square is another sort of workshop, - a place where jewelry is made by hand. The girl who does this work draws her own designs and executes them, and the results are infinitely quainter and more beautiful than the things to be bought at jewelry shops. She buys her copper and silver and the little gold she uses in bulk; her jewels - semi-precious stones for the most part - come from all over the world. In her cool, airy workroom with the green trees of the big Square outside, this little woman heats and bends and bores her metals and shines her stones in their quaint settings, with a rapt absorption that is balanced by her steady skill. It is no light or easy work, this making of hand-made jewelry, and it requires no inconsiderable gift of delicate fancy and artistic judgment. This girl is an artist, not the less so because she makes her flowers and dragons and symbolic figures out of metal instead of canvas and paint; not the less so because her colours do not come in tubes but imprisoned in the rare, exotic tints of shimmering gems.

Here is a ring of slightly dulled silver - the design is of a water lily, fragile and delicate. In the heart of it lies, like a dewdrop, a pale-green jewel called peridot. Here is the soft, rich blue of *lapis lazuli* - here the keener azure of turquoise matrix. Here is a Mexican opal, full of fire, almost blood-red, glowing feverishly from its burnished-copper setting. What a terrible, yet beautiful ornament! One would be, I imagine, under a sort of fierce and splendid spell while wearing it. Here, cool and pale and pure as a moonbeam, is a little water opal, - set in silver of course. Here is an "abalone blister," iridescent like mother-of-pearl, carrying in it something of "the shade and the shine of the sea" from which the mother-shell originally came. Here is matrix opal, and here are numbers of strange-hued, crystalline gems with names all ending in "ite." To model with metal for clay - to paint with jewels for colour! Does it not sound like very real and very fascinating art?

These are passing glimpses of but two of the art industries of the Village. There are many others - enough to fill a book all by themselves. There are the Villagers who hammer brass, and those who carve wood; who make exquisite lace, who make furniture of quaint and original design. There are the designers and decorators, whose brains are full of graceful images and whose fingers are quick and facile to carry them out. There are, in fact, numbers on numbers of enthusiastic young people - they are nearly all of them young - who from sunrise to sunset spend their lives in adding to the sum of beauty that there is on earth.

The making of box furniture, for instance, sounds commonplace enough, but it is really fascinating. There are places in the Village, - notably one on Greenwich Avenue, - where these clever craftsmen make wonderful things from cubic forms of wood, from boxes and sticks and laths and blocks. They can make anything from a desk to a tall candlestick, and, softly coloured, the square, wooden objects make a highly decorative effect. It is a simple art but a striking one, and the aesthetic sense, the instinct for balance and proportion and ultimate beauty of line and composition, has a splendid outlet.

There is, too, the trade of the designer of garments: the word is advisedly substituted for dresses. The real designer plans and executes pictures, mood-expressions, character settings. She dreams herself into the personalities of her clients, also the necessities and the limitations! Do you think all the artistic costume-creating is done in the Rue de la Paix? Try the Village!

And the florists! The flower shops of the Village are truly

lovely, one in particular, the Peculiar Flower Shop, which does not look at all like a shop but like the corner of a country garden. The Village loves flowers and understands them. Every Villager who can, grows them. Believe me, you know nothing about flowers in an intimate sense until you have talked with a flower-loving Villager!

Think of it - you outsiders who imagine that you are exhibiting a fine, artistic tendency by going to an occasional exhibition, and in knowing what colours can discreetly be worn together! Here is a small army of vigourous idealists who live, breathe and create beauty; whose happy, hard-working lives are filled with the exhilarating wine of art and artistic expression; who, when night comes, never turn the keys of their workshops without the knowledge that they have made one more beautiful thing since dawn, one more concrete materialisation of the art-dream in man, one more new creation to help to furnish pleasure for a beauty-loving world!

There is something about those new forms of art work which recalls the richer and more leisurely past, when good artisans were scarcely less revered than great artists; when men toiled half a lifetime to fashion one or two perfect things; when even the commonest utilitarian articles were expected to be beautiful and were made so by the applied genius of a race of working artists. It suggests other lands too - the East where you will hardly ever see an ugly object, and where everything from a pitcher to a rug is a thing of loveliness; the South where true grace of line and colour is the rule rather than the exception in the homeliest household utensils. Primitive peoples have always stayed close to beauty; it is odd that it has always remained for civilisation to suggest to man that if a thing is useful it need not necessarily be beautiful. In a sense, then, our Villagers have returned to a simpler, purer and surer standard. In shutting out the rest of Philistia they have also succeeded in shutting out Philistia's inconceivable ugliness. So the gods give them joy - the gods give them joy!

Probably no one region on earth has been more misrepresented and miswritten-up than the Village. Its eccentricities, harmless or otherwise, are sufficiently conspicuous to furnish targets both for the unscrupulous fiction-monger and the professional humourist. Sometimes when the fun is clever enough and true enough no one minds, the Village least of all; humour is their strong point. But they are quite subtle souls with all their child-like peculiarities; there is, in their acceptance of ridicule, a shrewd undercurrent suggestive of the "Virginian's" now classic warning: "When you call me that, *smile*!" Hence a novel written not long ago and purporting to be a mirror of the Village - Village life and Village ideals, or lack of them - had a peculiar result on the real Village. They knew it to be untrue - those few who read it, that is - but they scorned to notice it. They resented it, but to an astonishing extent they ignored it. The title of it got to mean very little to them save a general term of cheap and unmerited opprobrium, like some insulting epithet in a foreign language which one knows one would dislike if one could understand it. It is necessary to grasp these first simple facts to appreciate the following episode:

A certain young Villager - I shall not give his name, but he is an artist of growing and striking reputation, dark-eyed and rather attractive looking - burst into a friend's studio pale with anger:

"See here, have you a copy of 'The Trufflers'?"

"Not guilty," swore the surprised friend. "Why on earth do you want -"

But the young artist had dashed forth again, hot upon his quest. A few houses down the street, he made another spectacular entrance with the same cry; - at another and still another. One friend frankly confessed he had never heard of the book, another expressed indignation that he should be suspected of owning a copy. But not until the temperamental, brown-eyed artist had visited several acquaintances was he able to get what he wanted.

When the long-sought volume was in his grasp, he heaved a sigh of something more emphatic than relief.

"How much did you pay for this thing?" he demanded.

"I didn't. I borrowed it."

"Oh - See here. Can't you say you lost it?"

"I suppose so, if you want it as much as all that."

The young artist sat down and began seriously to tear the book to pieces.

"Well, for the love of Mike!" cried the friend. "Do you hate it like that?"

"I never read more than three pages of it," said the artist, steadily tearing, "but a slumming creature, a girl from uptown came into the 'Pirate's Den' yesterday where I was sitting, and, after staring at me fascinatedly for five minutes, leaned over to me and murmured breathlessly:

"'Oh, tell me, *aren't you a Truffler?*' I couldn't wring her neck, and so - "

Another handful of torn pages fluttered from his hand.

Of course, there are always the faddists and theorists, who take their ideals as hard as mumps or measles. Because the Village is so kind to new ideas, these flourish there for a time.

Here is a little tale told about a certain talented and charming lady who had a very complete set of theories and wished to try them out on Greenwich. One of her pet theories was that The People were naturally aesthetic; that The People's own untutored instinct would always unerringly select the best; that it was an insult to the noble idealism of The People to try to educate them; they were, so to speak, born with an education, ready-made, automatic, in sound working order from the beginning. Now, anyone almost may have theories, but if they are wise souls they won't try to apply them. If they have never been practically tested they can't be proved fallacious and thus may be treasured and loved and petted indefinitely, to the comfort of the individual and the edification of the multitude. But this fair idealist would not let well enough alone. She wanted to put her favourite theory to the acid test. So this is what she did.

In the one-time roadhouse on Washington Square was a saloon the name of which suggested an embryotic impulse toward poetry; or perhaps she picked that particular "pub" at random. At all events she walked into the bar, put her foot up on the traditional rail and began to converse with the barkeep.

She asked him if he had ever seen any of Shakespeare's plays, and he said no. She asked him if he would like to see one. He said sure - he'd try anything once. She invited him to go to see "Hamlet" with her, and he said he was game. Lest his sensitive feelings be hurt by finding himself a humble daw among the peacocks of the rich, gay world, she bought seats in the balcony and wore her shabbiest gown.

When he called for her she felt slightly faint. He was in evening dress, the most impeccable evening dress conceivable, even to the pumps and the opera hat. He, too, looked a little shocked when he saw her. Doubtless he would have asked her to dine at Rector's first if she had been properly dressed. They both recovered sufficiently to go to "Hamlet," and she trembled lest he would not like it. She need not have worried - or rather she had more cause to worry than she knew. Like it? He loved it; he shouted with honest mirth from first to last. And, when it was over -

"Say," he burst out, "that beats any musical comedy show hollow! *It's the funniest thing I ever see in my life!*"

Henceforward that dear lady did not let her theories out in a cold world, but kept them safe in cotton wool under lock and key.

There are fakers in the Village - just as there are fakers everywhere else. Only, of course, the ardour of new ideas which sincerely animates the Village does lend itself to all manner of poses. And because of this a perfectly earnest movement will attract a number of superficial dilettanti who dabble in it until it is in disrepute. And, vice versa, a crassly artificial fad will, by its novelty and picturesqueness, draw some of the real thinking people. Such inconsistencies and discrepancies are bound to occur in any such mental crucible as Greenwich. And, moreover, if the true and the false get a bit mixed once in a way, the wise traveller who goes to learn and not to sit in judgment will not look upon it to the disadvantage or the disparagement of the Village. Young, fervent and courageous souls may make a vast quantity of mistakes ere they be proved wrong with any sort of sound reasoning. If our Villagers run off at tangents on occasion, follow a few false gods and tie the cosmos into knots, it is, one may take it, rather to their credit than otherwise. No one ever accomplished anything by sitting still and looking at a wall. And it is far better to make a fool of yourself with an intense object, than to make nothing of yourself and have no particular object at all!

There are all sorts of fakers - conscious or otherwise. There is the futurist, post-impressionist *poseur* who more than half believes in his own pose. Possibly two small incidents may indicate what the genuine Villagers think of him.

There was once a post-impressionist exhibition at the Liberal Club, and a certain young man who shall be nameless was placed in charge of it. He was a perfectly sane young man and he knew that many of the "art specimens" hung on such occasions were flagrant frauds. Sketch after sketch, study after study, was sent in to him as master of ceremonies until, in his own words, he became so "fed up with post-impressionism that he could not stand another daub of the stuff!" The worm turned eventually, and he vowed to teach those "artists" a short, sweet lesson. He knew nothing about painting, being a writer by trade, but he had the run of several studios and could collect paint as he willed. After fortifying himself with a sufficiency of Dutch courage, he set up a canvas and painted a picture. It had no subject, no lines, no scheme, no integral idea. It was just a squareful of paint - and it held every shade and variety of paint that he could lay his hands on. He says that he took a wicked satisfaction in smearing the colours upon that desecrated canvas. His disgust with the futurist artists who had submitted their works for exhibition was one element to nerve his arm and fire his resentful spirit - another was the stimulus he had, in sheer desperation, wooed so recklessly. When the thing was done it was something for angels and devils alike to tremble before. It meant nothing, of course, but, like many inscrutable and unfathomable things, it terrified by its sheer blank, chaotic madness. He hung it in the exhibition. And it was - yes, it was - the hit of the occasion. This is not a fairy tale - not even fiction. The story was told me by the culprit - or was it genius? - himself.

And then people began to talk about it and speculate on what its real, inner meaning might be. They said it was a "mood picture," a "study in soul-tones" and a lot more like that. They even asked the guilty man what he thought of it. When he coldly responded that he thought it "looked like the devil" they told him that, of course he would say so: he had no soul for art.

Now, he had signed this horror, but (let me quote him): "I had signed it in a post-impressionist style, so no one on the earth could read the name."

After a few days an artist came along who was not wholly obsessed with the new craze. He studied the thing on the wall, and after a while he said: "Someone is guying you. That isn't a picture. It's a joke."

The futurist devotees were indignant, but there were enough

Anna Alice Chapin

who were stung by faint suspicion to investigate. They studied that signature upside down and under a microscope. After a while they got the identity of the man responsible for it, and - we draw a veil over the rest!

Then there was the man - another one - who, by way of a cheerful experiment, painted a post-impressionist picture with a billiard cue, jabbing gaily at the canvas as though trying to make difficult screwed shots, caroms and so on. Having done his worst in this way, he then took his picture to a gallery and exhibited it upside down. It attracted much attention and a fair quota of praise.

Stories such as these might discourage one if one did not keep remembering that even in far deeper and greater affairs of life, "A hair perhaps divides the false and true." Who are we to improve on Omar's wise and tolerant philosophy?

I have less sympathy with the girl who wrote poetry, and even occasionally sold it, at so much a line. Having sold a poem of eighteen lines for $9.00 she almost wept because, as she ingenuously complained, she might just as easily have written twenty lines for $10.00!

Then there is the fair Villager who intones Walt Whitman to music of her own composition; that is a bit trying, I grant you. And the male Villager who frequents spiritualistic seances and communes with dead poets.

One night Emerson presided. And, after the ghosts had departed, the spiritualistic Villager read some of his own poems.

"And do you know," he declared, enraptured, "everyone thought it was still Emerson who was speaking!"

Now for him we may have sympathy. He is perhaps a faker, but I am inclined to believe that he is that anachronism, a sincere faker. He is on the level. Like two-thirds of the Village, he is playing his game with his whole heart and soul, with all that is in him. I am afraid that it would be hard to say as much for a certain class of outside-the-Village fakers who, from time to time, drift into the cheery confines thereof and carry away sacks of shekels - though not, let us hope, as much as they wanted to get!

Have you ever heard, for instance, of the psychoanalysts? They diagnose soul troubles as regular doctors diagnose diseases of the body, and they are in great demand. Some of them are alienists, healers of sick brains; some of them are just - fakers. They charge immense prices, and just for the moment the blessed Village - always passionately hospitable to new cults and theories and visions - is receiving them cordially, with arms and purses that are both wide open.

None of us can afford to depreciate the genius nor the judgment of Freud, but I defy any Freud-alienist to efficiently psychoanalyse the Village! By the time he were half done with the job he would be a Villager himself and then - pouf! That for his psychoanalysis!

Have you ever read that most enchanting book of Celtic mysticism, inconsequent whimsey and profound symbolism - "The Crock of Gold" - by one James Stevens? The author is not a Villager, and his message is one which has its root and spring in the signs and wonders of another, an older and a more intimately wise land than ours. But when I read of those pure, half-pagan immortals in the dance of the *Sluaige Shee* (the Fairy Hosts) I could not help thinking that Greenwich Village might well adopt certain passages as fitting texts and interpretations of themselves and their own lives - "The lovers of gaiety and peace, long defrauded."

The Shee, as they dance, sing to the old grey world-dwellers, - or Stevens says they do, and I for one believe he knows all there is to know about it ('tis a Leprechaun he has for a friend):

Anna Alice Chapin

"Come to us, ye who do not know where ye are - ye who live among strangers in the houses of dismay and self-righteousness. Poor, awkward ones! How bewildered and be-devilled ye go!... In what prisons are ye flung? To what lowliness are ye bowed? How are ye ground between the laws and the customs? Come away! For the dance has begun lightly, the wind is sounding over the hill...."

# CHAPTER IX

## AND THEN MORE VILLAGERS

... A meeting place for the few who are struggling ever and ever for an art that will be truly American. An art that is not hidebound by the deadening influences of a decadent Europe, or the result of intellectual theories evolved by those whose only pleasure in existence is to create laws for others to obey ... an art, let us say, that springs out of the emotional depths of creative spirit, courageous and unafraid of rotting power, or limited scope ... an art whose purpose is flaming beauty of creation and nothing else.

- HAROLD HERSEY, in *The Quill* (Greenwich Village).

Someone said today to the author of this book:

"How can you write about the Village? You don't live here. Live here a few years and then perhaps you'll have something to say!"

It is by way of answer that the following little tale is quoted; it is an old tale but, after a fashion, it seems to fit.

Once upon a time an explorer discovered a country and set about to write a book concerning it. Then the people of the country became somewhat indignant and asked:

"Why should a stranger, who has scarcely learned his way about in our land, attempt to describe it? We, who have lived in it and know it, will write its chronicles ourselves."

So the traveller sat down and shut the book in which he had begun to write and said:

"Well and good. Do you write about your country, the land you have lived in so long and know so well, and we will see what we shall see."

So the people of the country - or their scribes, a most gifted company - began the task of describing that which they knew and loved, and had lived in and with since birth. And after they were through they took the fruits of their joint labours to an assemblage of kings in a far-off place.

And the kings said, after they had read:

"This is beautiful literature, but what is the country like, - that of which they write?"

So one of their chamberlains, who was a plain soul, said sensibly:

"Your Majesties, there is only one fault to find with the book written by these people about their country, and that is that they know it too well to describe it well."

Therefore one of the kings said, "How can that be truth? For what we are close to we must see more clearly than others who view it from afar."

So the sensible chamberlain took a certain little object and held it close to the eyes of one of the kings, and cried, "What is this?"

And the king, blinking and scowling, said after a bit:

"It is a volcano!"

The chamberlain answered, "Wrong; it is an inkstand," and showing it proved that he spoke truth.

Then he held another thing close before the eyes of another king and cried again, "What is this?"

And this king, puzzled, said, "I think it is a little piece of cloth."

"Wrong," said the sensible chamberlain. "It is the statue of the Winged Victory."

And this happened not once but many times until at length the kings understood. And they made a law that no one should stand too close to the thing he wished to see clearly. And they added their judgment that only the visitors to a country could see it as it is.

So the traveller dipped his quill in ink once more and started writing his book. It is not yet known how successful he was.

Travellers make terrible errors, and yet at times they bring back fragments of truth that the natives of the land have left unheeded scattered on the soil of the countryside. Sometimes their fragments prove to be useless and without value, for there are travellers and travellers, and some will be as stupid and as blind as the rest are clever. If this book turns out to be written by one of the stupid travellers - try to be generous, you Villagers - but then the Village is always generous!

The studio life of Greenwich is really and truly as primitive, as picturesque, as poverty-stricken and as gaily adventurous as the story-tellers say. People really do live in big, quaint, bare rooms with scarcely enough to buy the necessaries of life; and they are undoubtedly gay in the doing of it. There is a sort of *camaraderie* among the "Bohemians" of the world below Fourteenth Street which the more restricted uptowners find it hard to believe in. It is difficult for those uptowners to

Anna Alice Chapin

understand a condition of mind which makes it possible for a number of ambitious young people in a studio building to go fireless and supperless one day and feast gloriously the next; to share their rare windfalls without thought of obligation on any side; to burn candles instead of kerosene in order to dine at "Polly's"; to borrow each other's last pennies for books or pictures or drawing materials, knowing that they will all go without butter or milk for tomorrow's breakfast.

If one is hard up, one expects to be offered a share in someone's good fortune; if one has had luck oneself, one expects, as a matter of course, to share it. Such is the code of the studios.

Anabel, for example, is sitting up typing her newest poem at 1 A.M. when a knock comes on the studio door. She opens it to confront the man who lives on the top floor and whom she has never met. She hasn't the least idea what his name is. He carries a tea caddy, a teapot and a teacup.

"Sorry," he explains casually, "but I saw your light, and I thought you'd let me use your gas stove to make some tea. Mine is out of commission. Just go ahead with your work, while I fuss about. Maybe you'd take a cup when it's ready?"

Anabel does, and he retires, cheerfully unconscious of anything unconventional in the episode.

"Jimmy," calls Louise, the fashion illustrator, from the front door, one day, "I have to have two dollars to pay my gas bill. Got any?"

"One-sixty," floats down a voice from upstairs.

"Chuck it down, please. I'll be getting some pay tomorrow, and we can blow it in."

So Jimmy chucks it down. Louise is a nice girl, and would merrily "chuck" him the same amount if she happened to have it. That's all there is to it.

There is a great deal of nonsense talked about the wickedness or at least the impropriety of Greenwich Village - and some of the talk is by people who ought to know better. The Village is, to be sure, entirely unconventional and incurably romantic and dramatic in its tastes. It is appallingly honest, dangerously young in spirit and it is rather too intense sometimes, keyed up unduly with ambition and emotion and the eagerness of living. But wicked? Not a bit of it!

And the heavenly, inconsequent, infectious, absurd gaiety of it!

The Lady Who Owns the Parrot (Pollypet is the bird's name) appears in a new hat; a gorgeous, new hat, with a band of scarlet and green feathers.

"Whence the more than Oriental splendour?" demands in surprise the Poet from the Third Floor, who knows that the Lady is not patronising Fifth Avenue shops at present.

"Pollypet is moulting!" explains the Lady of the Parrot, with a laugh.

Dear, merry, kindly, pitiful life of the studios! - irresponsible, perhaps, and not of vast economic importance, but so human and so enchanting; so warm when it is bitter cold, so rich when the larder is empty, so gay when disappointment and failure are sitting wolf-like at the door.

A rich woman who loves the Village and often-times goes down there to buy her gifts rather than get them from the more conservative places uptown, told me that once when she went to a Village gift-shop to purchase a number of presents, she found the proprietor away. She was asked to pick out what she wanted, and make a list. She did. Nobody even questioned her accuracy. The next time she went she had a friend with her, who was, I imagine, more or less thrilled by the notion of approaching the bad, bold city, - she was from out of town.

The shopkeeper was out in the back garden dressed in blue overalls and shirt, hoeing vigorously.

"Is this the heart of Bohemia?" demanded the astonished provincial.

After their purchases were made and done up, they wanted twine. Don't forget, please, that this was a shop.

"Twine?" murmured the picturesque proprietor gently. "Of course I should have some; I must remember to get some twine!"

The sympathies are always ready there, the pennies too, when there are any! A lame man, a sick woman, a little child, a forlorn dog or cat, - they have only to go and sit on the steps of one of those blessed studio buildings, to receive pity, help and cheer. And - ye gods! - isn't the fact well known! And isn't it taken advantage of, just! The swift, unreasoning charity of these Bohemians is so well recognised that it is a regular graft for the unscrupulous.

But they keep right on being cheated right and left; thank heaven, they will never learn to be wiser!

This difference between the Village view and the conventional standpoint is very difficult to analyse. It really can only be made clear by examples. As, for instance:

It is fairly late in the evening. In one of the little tea shops is a group of girls and men smoking. To them enters a youth, who is hailed with "How is Dickey's neuralgia?"

The newcomer grins and answers: "Better, I guess. He's had six drinks, and is now asleep upstairs on Eleanore's couch. He'll be all right when he wakes up."

They laugh, but quite sympathetically, and the subject is dismissed.

Now, there is a noteworthy point in this trifling episode, though it may appear a trifle obscure at first. There is, to be sure, nothing especially interesting or edifying in the fact of a young man's drinking himself into insensibility to dull a faceache; the thing has been known before. Neither is it an unheard-of occurrence for a friendly and charitably inclined woman to grant him harbour room till he has slept it off. The only striking point about this is that it is taken so entirely as a matter of course by the Villagers. It no more astonishes them that Eleanore should give up her couch to a male acquaintance for an indefinite number of night hours, than that she should give him a cup of tea. It is entirely the proper, kindly thing to do; if Eleanore had not done it, she would not be a Villager, and the Village would have none of her.

It may be further remarked that, if you should go upstairs to Eleanore's studio, you would find that she takes the presence on the couch as calmly as though it were a bundle of laundry. She is in no sense disconcerted by the occasional snore that wakes the midnight echoes. She works peacefully on at the black-and-white poster which she is going to submit tomorrow. She does not resent Dickey at all. Neither does she watch his slumbers tenderly nor hover over him in the approved manner. Eleanore is not the least bit sentimental, - few Villagers are. They are merely romantic and kindly, which are different and sturdier graces.

Toward morning Dickey will wake and Eleanore will make him black coffee and send him home. And there will be the end of that.

Conceive such a situation on the outside! Imagine the feminine flutter of the conventional Julia. Fancy, above all, the hungry gossip of conventional Julia's conventional friends! But in the Village there is very little scandal, and practically no slander. They are very slow to think evil.

And this in spite of their rather ridiculous way of talking. They do, a number of them, give the uninitiated an impression of moral laxity. Their phrases, "the free relation," "the rights of sex," "suppressed desires," "love without bonds," "liberty of the individual" do, when jumbled up sufficiently, make a composite picture of strange and lurid aspect. But actually, they are not one atom less moral than any other group of human beings, - in fact, thanks to their unquestionable ideals and their habit of fearless thinking, they are, I think, a good bit more so.

"While I lived in the Village," writes one shrewd man, "I heard of more impropriety and saw less of it than anywhere I've ever been!"

Here is another glimpse:

The casual visitor to one of the basement "shops" climbs down the steep steps and pauses at the door to look at the picture. It is rather early, and only two customers have turned up so far. They are sitting in deep, comfortable chairs smoking and drinking (as usual, ginger-ale). One of the proprietors - a charmingly pretty girl - is sweeping, preparatory to the evening "trade." When her husband comes in she is going to leave him in charge and go to the Liberal Club for a dance, so she is exquisitely dressed in a peach-coloured gown, open of neck and short of sleeve. She is slim and graceful and her bright-brown hair is cropped in the Village mode. She is the most attractive maid-of-all-work that the two "customers" have ever seen. When, pausing in her labours, she offers them her own cigarette case with the genuine simplicity and grace of a child offering sweetmeats, their subjugation is complete. Though they are strangers in a strange land - they have only dropped in to find out an address of a friend who lives in the Village - they never misunderstand the situation, their hostess nor the atmosphere for a moment. No one misunderstands the charming, picturesque _camaraderie_ of the Village - unless they have been reading Village novelists, that breed held in contempt by Harry Kemp and all the Greenwichers. Anyone who goes there with an open mind will carry it away filled with nothing but good things - save sometimes perhaps a little envy.

And, by the bye, that habit of calling at strange places to locate people is emphatically a Village custom. Or rather, perhaps, it should be put the other way: the habit of giving some "shop" or eating place instead of a regular address is most prevalent among Villagers. A Villager is seldom in his own quarters unless he has a shop of his own. But if he really "belongs" he is known to hundreds of other people, and the enquiring caller will be passed along from one place to another, until, in time, he will be almost certain to locate his nomadic friend.

"Billy Robinson? Why, yes, of course, we know him. No, he hasn't been in tonight. But you try some of the other places that he goes to. He's very apt to drop in at the 'Klicket' during the evening. Or if he isn't there try 'The Mad Hatter's,' - 'Down the Rabbit Hole' you know; - or let's see - he'll be sure to show up at the Club some time before midnight. If you don't find him come back here; maybe he'll drop in later, or else someone will who has seen him."

Of course, he is found eventually, - usually quite soon, for the Village is a small place, and a true Village in its neighbourliness and its readiness to pass a message along.

Really, there is nothing quainter about it than this intimate and casual quality, such as is known in genuine, small country towns. Fancy a part of New York City - Gotham, the cold, the selfish, the unneighbourly, the indifferent - in which everyone knows everyone else and takes a personal interest in them too; where distances are slight and pleasant, where young men in loose shirts with rolled-up sleeves, or girls hatless and in working smocks stroll across Sixth Avenue from one square to another with as little self-consciousness as though they were meandering down Main Street to a game of tennis or the village store! Sixth Avenue, indeed, has come to mean nothing more to them than a rustic bridge or a barbed-wire fence, - something to be gotten over speedily and forgotten. They even, by some alchemy of view point, seem to give it a rural air from Jefferson Market down to Fourth Street - these cool-looking, hatless young people who make their leisurely way

Anna Alice Chapin

down Washington Place or along Fourth Street. People pass them, - people in hats, coats and carrying bundles; but the Villagers do not notice them. They do not even look at them pityingly; they do not look at them at all. Your true Green-Village denizen does not like to look at unattractive objects if he can possibly avoid it.

Of course, they do make use of Sixth Avenue occasionally, on their rare trips uptown. But it is in the same spirit that a country dweller would take the railway in order to get into the city on necessary business. As a matter of fact there is no corner of New York more conveniently situated for transportation than this particular section of Greenwich. I came across a picturesque real estate advertisement the other day:

> "If you ever decide to kill your barber and fly the country, commit the crime at the corner of Eighth Street and Sixth Avenue. There is probably no other place in the world that offers as many avenues of flight."

But nothing short of dire necessity ever takes a Villager uptown. He, or she, may go downtown but not up. Uptown nearly always means something distasteful and boring to the Village; they see to it that they have as few occasions for going there as possible.

Anyway, uptown, for them, ends very far downtown! The fifties, forties, thirties, even the twenties, are to them the veritable wilderness, the variously repugnant sections of relatively outer darkness.

Do you remember Colonel Turnbull who had so much trouble in selling his house at Eighth Street because it was so far out of town? Here is a modern and quite surprisingly neat analogy:

Two Village women of my acquaintance met the other day. Said one tragically: "My dear, isn't it awful? We've had to move uptown! Since the baby came, we need a larger house, but it almost breaks my heart!"

"I should think so!" gasped the second woman in consternation. "You've always been such regular Villagers. What shall we do without you? It's terrible! Where are you moving to, dear?"

"- West Eleventh Street!" sobbed the sad, prospective exile.

There are Villagers who while scarcely celebrities are characters so well known, locally, as to stand out in bizarre relief even against that variegated background of personalities. There is Doris, the dancer, slim, strange, agile, with a genius for the centre of the Bohemian stage, an expert, exotic style of dancing, and a singular and touching passion for her only child. At the Greenwich masquerades she used to shine resplendent, her beautiful, lithe body glorious with stage-jewels, and not much else; for the time being she has flitted away, but some day she will surely return like a darkly brilliant butterfly, and the Village will again thrill to her dancing. There is Hyppolite, the anarchist, dark and fervid; there is "Bobby" Edwards, the Village troubadour, with his self-made and self-decorated *ukelele*, and his cat, Dirty Joe; there is Charlie-immortal barber! - whose trade is plied in sublime accordance with Village standards, and whose "ad" runs as follows:

> "The only barber shop in the Village where work is done conforming to its ideals.... Four barbers in attendance supervised by the popular boy-proprietor - CHARLIE."

There is Peggy, the artist's model, who has posed for almost every artist of note, and who is as pretty as a pink carnation.

There is Tiny Tim - of immense proportions - who keeps the Tiny Tim Candy Shop; an impressive person who carries trays of candy about the Village, and who swears that he has sweets to match your every mood.

"If they don't express your character, I'll take them back!" he declares. Though how he could take them back.... However, in the Village you need not be too exact. There is "Ted" Peck's Treasure Box. Here all manner of charming things are sold; and here Florence Beales exhibits her most exquisite studies in photography.

There is the strong-minded young woman, who is always starting clubs; there is the Osage Indian who speaks eight languages and draws like a god; there are a hundred and one familiar spirits of the Village, eccentric, inasmuch as they are unlike the rest of the world, but oh, believe me, a goodly company to have as neighbours.

People have three mouthpieces, three vehicles of expression, besides their own lips. We are not talking now about that self-expression which is to be found in individual act or word in any form. We are speaking in a more practical and also a more social sense. In this sense we may cite three distinct ways in which a community may become articulate: through its press; through its clubs or associations; through its entertainments and social life. Greenwich has a number of magazines, an even larger number of clubs and an unconscionable number of ways of entertaining itself - from theatrical companies to balls!

Of course the best known of the Greenwich magazines is *The Masses*, owned by Max Eastman and edited by Floyd Dell. It has, in a sense, grown beyond the Village, inasmuch as it now circulates all over the country, wherever socialistic or anarchistic tendencies are to be found. But its inception was in Greenwich Village, and in its infant days it strongly reflected the radical, young, insurgent spirit which was just beginning to ferment in the world below Fourteenth Street. In those days it was poor and struggling too (as is altogether fitting in a Village paper) and lost nothing in freshness and spontaneity and vigour from that fact.

"You might tell," said Floyd Dell, with a twinkle, "of the days when *The Masses* was in Greenwich Avenue, and the editor, the business manager and the stenographer played ball in the street all day long!"

It is, perhaps, symbolic that *The Masses* in moving uptown stopped at Fourteenth Street, the traditional and permanent boundary line. There it may reach out and touch the great world, yet still remain part of the Village where it was born.

Here is one man's views of the Liberal Club. I am half afraid to quote them, they sound so heretical, but I wish to emphasise the fact that they are quoted. They might be the snapping of the fox at the sour grapes for all I know! Though this particular man seemed calm and dispassionate. "The Liberal Club Board," he said, "is a purely autocratic institution. It is collectively a trained poodle, though composed of nine members. The procedure is to make a few long speeches, praise the club, and re-elect the Board. Perfectly simple. But - did you say *Liberal* Club?" He used to sit on the Board himself, too!

A visiting Scotch socialist proclaimed it, without passion, a "hell of a place," and some of its most striking anarchistic leaders, "vera interestin' but terrible damn fools"! But he was, doubtless, an eccentric though an experienced and dyed-in-the-wool socialist who had lectured over half the globe. It is recorded of him that once when a certain young and energetic Village editor had been holding forth uninterruptedly and dramatically for an hour on the rights of the working-man, etc., etc., the visiting socialist, who had been watching his fervent gesticulations with absorbed attention, suddenly leaned forward and seized the lapel of his coat.

"Mon!" he exclaimed earnesly, "do ye play tennis?"

Just what is the Liberal Club?

You may have contradictory answers commensurate with the number of members you interrogate. One will tell you that it is a fake; one that it is the only vehicle of free speech; Arthur Moss says it is "the most *il*-liberal club in the world"! Floyd

Dell says it is paramountly a medium for entertainment, and that it is "not so much a clearing house of new ideas as of new people"!

The Liberal Club goes up, and the Liberal Club goes down. It has its good seasons and its bad, its fluctuations as to standards and favour, its share in the curious and inevitable tides that swing all associations back and forth like pendulums.

There is a real passion for dancing in the Village, and it is beautiful dancing that shows practice and a natural sense of rhythm. The music may be only from a victrola or a piano in need of tuning, but the spirit is, most surely, the vital spirit of the dance. At the Liberal Club everyone dances. After you have passed through the lounge room - the conventional outpost of the club, with desks and tables and chairs and prints and so on - you find yourself in a corridor with long seats, and windows opening on to Nora Van Leuwen's big, bare, picturesque Dutch Oven downstairs. On the other side of the corridor is the dance room - also the latest exhibition. Some of the pictures are very queer indeed. The last lot I saw were compositions in deadly tones of magenta and purple. The artist was a tall young man, the son of a famous illustrator. He strolled in quite tranquilly for a dance, - with those things of his in full view! All the courage is not on battlefields.

Said a girl, who, Village-like, would not perjure her soul to be polite:

"Why so much magenta?"

And said he quite sweetly:

"Why not? I can paint people green if I like, can't I?"

With which he glided imperturbably off in a fox trot with a girl in an "art sweater."

Harry Kemp says: "They make us sick with their scurrilous,

ignorant stories of the Village. Pose? Sure! - it's two-thirds pose. But the rest is beautiful. And even the pose is beautiful in its way. Life is rotten and beautiful both at once. So is the Village. The Village is big in idea and it's growing. They talk of its being a dead letter. It's just beginning. First it - the Village, as it is now - was really a sort of off-shoot of London and Paris. Now it's itself and I tell you it's beautiful, and more remarkable than people know.

"Uptowners, outsiders, come in here and insist on getting in; and, fed on the sort of false stuff that goes out through 'novelists' and 'reporters,' think that anything will go in the Liberal Club! They come here and insult the women members, and we all end up in a free fight every week or so. All the fault of the writers who got us wrong in the first place, and handed on the wrong impression to the world...."

The studio quarters of the Village are located in various places - the South Side of Washington Square, the little lost courts and streets and corners everywhere, and - Macdougal Alley, Washington Mews, and the new, rather stately structures on Eighth Street, which are almost too grand for real artists and yet which have attracted more than a few nevertheless. I suppose that the Alley, - jutting off from the famous street named for Alexander Macdougal, - is the best known.

I remember that once, some years ago, I was hurrying, by a short cut, from Eighth Street to Waverly Place, and saw something which made me stop short in amazement. As unexpectedly as though it had suddenly sprung there, I beheld a little street running at right angles from me, parallel with Eighth, but ending, like a *cul de sac*, in houses like those with which it was edged. It was a quaint and foreign-looking little street and seemed entirely out of place in New York, - and especially out of place plunged like that into the middle of a block.

But that was not the oddest part of it. In that street stood talking a girl in gorgeous Spanish dress and a man in Moorish costume. The warm reds and greens and russets of their garments made an unbelievable patch of colour in the grey March day. And this in New York!

A friendly truck driver, feeding his horses, saw my bewilderment, and laughed.

"That's Macdougal's Alley," he volunteered.

That meant nothing to me then.

"What is it?" I demanded, devoured by curiosity; "the stage door of a theatre, - or what?"

He laughed again.

"It is just Macdougal's Alley!" he repeated, as though that explained everything.

So it did, when I came to find out about it.

The Alley and Washington Mews are probably the most famous artist quarters in the city, and some of our biggest painters and sculptors once had studios in one or the other, - those, that is, that haven't them still. Of course the picturesquely attired individuals I had caught sight of were models - taking the air, or snatching a moment for flirtation. Naturally they would not have appeared in costume in any other street in New York, but this, you see, was Macdougal Alley, and as my friend, the truck driver, seemed to think, that explains everything!

As for the Mews, they are fixing it up in great shape; and as for those Eighth-Street studios, they are too beautiful for words. You look out on Italian gardens, and you know that you are nowhere near New York, with its prose and drudgery. If for a moment it seems all a bit too perfect for the haphazard, inspirational loveliness of the Village, you will surely have an arresting instinct which will tell you that it is just consummating a Village dream; it is just making what every Villager lives to make come true: perfect artistic beauty.

As we have seen, dancing is a real passion in the Village. So we can scarcely leave it without touching on the "Village dances" which have been so striking a feature of recent times and have proved so useful and so fruitful to the tired Sunday-supplement newspaperman. There are various sorts, from the regular pageants staged by the Liberal Club and the Kit Kat, to those of more modest pretensions given by individual Villagers or groups of Villagers.

The *Quatres Arts* balls of Paris doubtless formed the basis for these affairs; indeed, a description given me years ago by William Dodge, the artist, might almost serve as the story of one of these Village balls today. And Doris, who, I believe, appeared on one occasion as "Aphrodite," - in appropriate "costume" - recalls the celebrated model Sara Brown who electrified Paris by her impersonation of "Cleopatra" at a *"Quatz 'Arts"* gathering, - somewhat similarly arrayed, - or should we say decorated?

The costumes, - many of them at least, - are largely - paint! This is not nearly as improper as it sounds. Splashes of clever red and subtle purple will quite creditably take the place of more cumberous and expensive dressing, - or at least will pleasantly eke it out. Colour has long been recognised as a perfectly good substitute for cloth. Have you forgotten the small boy's abstract of the first history book -" ... The early Britons wore animals' skins in winter, and in summer they painted themselves blue." I am convinced that wode was the forerunner of the dress of the Village ball!

The Kit Kat, an artists' association, is remarkable for one curious custom. Its managing board is a profound mystery. No one knows who is responsible for the invitations sent out, so there can be no jealousy nor rancour if people don't get asked. If an invited guest chooses to bring a friend he may, but he is solely responsible for that friend and if his charge proves undesirable he will be held accountable and will thereafter be quietly dropped from the guest list of subsequent balls. And still he will never know who has done it! Hence, the Kit Kat is a most formidable institution, and invitations from its mysterious "Board" are hungrily longed for!

Every season there are other balls, too; among the last was the "Apes and Ivory" affair, a study in black and white, as may be gathered; then there was the "Rogue's Funeral" ball. This was to commemorate the demise of a certain little magazine called the *Rogue*, whose career was short and unsuccessful. They kept the funeral atmosphere so far as to hire a hearse for the transportation of some of the guests, *but* -

"We put the first three letters of funeral in capitals," says one of the participants casually.

The proper thing, when festivities are over, is to go to breakfast, - at "Polly's," the Village Kitchen or the Dutch Oven, perhaps. Of course, nothing on earth but the resiliency, the electric vitality of youth, could stand this sort of thing; but then, the Village is young; it is preeminently the land of youth, and the wine of life is still fresh and strong enough in its veins to come buoyantly through what seems to an older consciousness a good bit more like an ordeal than an amusement!

And yet - and yet - somehow I cannot think that these balls and pageants and breakfasts are truly typical of the real Village - I mean the newest and the best Village - the Village which, like the Fairy Host, sings to the sojourners of the grey world to come and join them in their dance, with "the wind sounding over the hill." My Village is something fresher and gayer and more child-like than that. There is in it nothing of decadence.

But, as John Reed says -

"... *There's anaemia*
*Ev'n in Bohemia,*

*That there's not more of it - _ there _is the miracle!"*

For still the Village is, or has been, inarticulate. Individually it has found speech - it has expressed itself in diverse and successful forms. But there remains a void of voices! A community must strongly utter something, and must find mouths and mouthpieces for the purpose. It was hard to find, hard to locate, hard to vocalise, this message of the Village; eventually it came up from the depths and pitched its tone bravely and sweetly, so that men might hear and understand.

The need was for something concrete and yet varied, which could cry out alone, - a delicious voice in the wilderness, if you like! There have been play-acting companies, "The Washington Square Players," "The Provincetown Players," and others. But something was still wanting.

Sometimes it strikes us that wonderful things happen haphazard like meteors and miracles. But I believe if we could take the time to investigate, we would find that most of these miraculous and glorious oaks grow out of a quiet commonplace acorn.

Richard Wagner once held an idea - perhaps it would better be termed an ideal - concerning art expression. He declared (you may read it in *"Oper und Drama"* unless you are too war-sided) that all the art forms belonged together: that no one branch of the perfect art form could live apart from its fellows, that is, in its integral parts. He contended (and enforced in Bayreuth) that all the arts were akin: that the brains which created music, drama, colour effects, plastic sculptural effects - anything and everything that belonged to artistic expression - were, or should be, welded into one supreme artistic expression. He believed this implicitly, and like other persons who believe well enough, he "got away with it." In Bayreuth, he established for all time a form of synthetic art which has never been rivalled.

Now Wagner has very little apparently to do with Greenwich Village. And yet this big world-notion is gaining way there.

Anna Alice Chapin

They are finding - as anyone must have known they would find - a new mood expression, a new voice. And, wise, not in their generation, but in all the generations, the Village has seized on this new vehicle with characteristic energy.

The new Greenwich Village Theatre which Mrs. Sam Lewis is godmothering, is - unless many sensible and farseeing persons are much mistaken - going to be the new Voice of the Village. It is going to express what the Villagers themselves are working for, day and night: beauty, truth, liberty, novelty, drama. It is going, in its theatrical form, to fill the need for something concrete and yet various, something involving all, yet evolved from all; something which shall somehow unite all the scattered rainbow filaments of Our Village into a lovely texture with a design that even a Philistine world can understand.

"Young, new American playwrights first," says Mrs. Lewis. "After that as many great plays of all kinds as we can find. But we want to open the channel for expression. We want to give the Village a voice."

And when she says the Village she does not mean just the section technically known as Greenwich. She means - I take it - that greater neighbourhood of the world, which is fervently concerned in the new and thrilling and wonderful and untrammelled things of life. They have no place to sing, out in the every-day world, but in the Village they are going to be heard.

And I think the new Greenwich Village Theatre is going to be one of their most resonant mouthpieces!

# A LAST WORD

And after all this, - what of the Village? Just what is it?

"In my experience," said the writing man of sententious sayings, "there have been a dozen 'villages.' The Village changes are like the waves of the sea!"

Interrogated further, he mentioned various phases which Greenwich had known. The studio-and-poverty Bohemian epoch, the labour and anarchy era, the futurist fad, the "free love" cult, the Bohemian-and-masquerade-ball period, the psychoanalysis craze; the tea-shop epidemic, the arts-and-crafts obsession, the play-acting mania; and other violent and more or less transient enthusiasms which had possessed the Village during the years he had lived there. Not wholly transient, he admitted. Something of each and all of them had remained - had stuck - as he expressed it. The Village assimilates ideas with miraculous speed; it gobbles them up, gets strong and well on the diet, and asks for more. It is so eager for novelty and new ideals and new view-points that if nothing entirely virgin comes along, it will take something quite old, and give it a new twist and adopt it with Village-like ardour.

Oh, you mustn't laugh at the Village, you wise uptowners, - or if you laugh it must be very, very gently and kindly, as you laugh at children; and rather reverently, too, in the knowledge that in lots of essentials the children know ever so much more than you do!

Anna Alice Chapin

It is true that changes do come over the Village like the waves of the sea, even as my friend said. But they are colourful waves, prismatic waves, fresh, invigourating and energetic waves, carrying on their crests iridescent seaweed and glittering shells and now and then a pearl. The Village has its treasure, have no doubt of that; never a phase touches it but leaves it the richer for the contact.

You, too, going down into this port o' dreams will win something of the wealth that is of the heart and soul and mind. You will come away with the sense of wider horizons and deeper penetrations than you knew before. You will find novel colours in the work-a-day world and a sort of quaint music in the song of the city. Some of the glowing reds and greens and purples that you saw those grown-up children in the Village joyously splashing on their wooden toys or the walls of their absurd and charming "shops" will somehow get into the grey fabric of your life; and a certain eager urging undertone of idealism and hope and sturdy aspiration will make you restless as you follow your common round. Perhaps you will go back. Perhaps you will keep it as a rainbow memory, a visualisation of the make-believe country where anything is possible. But in any case you will not forget.

Many a place gets into your mind and creates nostalgia when you are far from it. But Greenwich Village gets into your heart, and you will never be quite able to lose the magic of it all the days of your life.

# Choose from Thousands of 1stWorldLibrary Classics By

A. M. Barnard
Ada Leverson
Adolphus William Ward
Aesop
Agatha Christie
Alexander Aaronsohn
Alexander Kielland
Alexandre Dumas
Alfred Gatty
Alfred Ollivant
Alice Duer Miller
Alice Turner Curtis
Alice Dunbar
Ambrose Bierce
Amelia E. Barr
Amory H. Bradford
Andrew Lang
Andrew McFarland Davis
Andy Adams
Anna Sewell
Annie Besant
Annie Hamilton Donnell
Annie Payson Call
Annonaymous
Anton Chekhov
Arnold Bennett
Arthur Conan Doyle
Arthur M. Winfield
Arthur Ransome
Atticus
B.H. Baden-Powell
B. M. Bower
Baroness Emmuska Orczy
Baroness Orczy
Basil King
Bayard Taylor
Ben Macomber
Bertha Muzzy Bower
Bjornstjerne Bjornson
Booth Tarkington
Boyd Cable
Bram Stoker
C. Collodi
C. E. Orr
C. M. Ingleby
Carolyn Wells
Catherine Parr Traill
Charles A. Eastman
Charles Dickens

Charles Dudley Warner
Charles Farrar Browne
Charles Ives
Charles Kingsley
Charles Klein
Charles Amory Beach
Charles Hanson Towne
Charles Lathrop Pack
Charles Whibley
Charles Willing Beale
Charlotte M. Braeme
Charlotte M. Yonge
Charlotte Perkins Stetson
Clair W. Hayes
Clarence Day Jr.
Clarence E. Mulford
Clemence Housman
Confucius
Cornelis DeWitt Wilcox
Cyril Burleigh
D. H. Lawrence
Daniel Defoe
David Garnett
Dinah Craik
Don Carlos Janes
Donald Keyhoe
Dorothy Kilner
Dougan Clark
Douglas Fairbanks
E. Nesbit
E.P.Roe
E. Phillips Oppenheim
Earl Barnes
Edgar Rice Burroughs
Edith Van Dyne
Edith Wharton
Edward J. O'Biren
Edward S. Ellis
Edwin L. Arnold
Eleanor Atkins
Eliot Gregory
Elizabeth Gaskell
Elizabeth McCracken
Elizabeth Von Arnim
Ellem Key
Emerson Hough
Emilie F. Carlen
Emily Dickinson
Enid Bagnold

Enilor Macartney Lane
Erasmus W. Jones
Ernie Howard Pie
Ethel Turner
Ethel Watts Mumford
Eugenie Foa
Eugene Wood
Eustace Hale Ball
Evelyn Everett-green
Everard Cotes
F. H. Cheley
F. J. Cross
Federick Austin Ogg
Ferdinand Ossendowski
Francis Bacon
Francis Darwin
Frances Hodgson Burnett
Frances Parkinson Keyes
Frank Gee Patchin
Frank Harris
Frank Jewett Mather
Frank L. Packard
Frank V. Webster
Frederic Stewart Isham
Frederick Trevor Hill
Frederick Winslow Taylor
Friedrich Kerst
Friedrich Nietzsche
Fyodor Dostoyevsky
G.A. Henty
G.K. Chesterton
Gabrielle E. Jackson
Garrett P. Serviss
Gaston Leroux
George A. Warren
George Ade
Geroge Bernard Shaw
George Durston
George Ebers
George Eliot
George Gissing
George MacDonald
George Meredith
George Orwell
George Sylvester Viereck
George Tucker
George W. Cable
George Wharton James
Gertrude Atherton

Grace E. King
Grace Gallatin
Grant Allen
Guillermo A. Sherwell
Gulielma Zollinger
Gustav Flaubert
H. A. Cody
H. B. Irving
H.C. Bailey
H. G. Wells
H. H. Munro
H. Irving Hancock
H. Rider Haggard
H. W. C. Davis
Hamilton Wright Mabie
Hans Christian Andersen
Harold Avery
Harold McGrath
Harriet Beecher Stowe
Harry Houidini
Helent Hunt Jackson
Helen Nicolay
Hendrik Conscience
Hendy David Thoreau
Henri Barbusse
Henrik Ibsen
Henry Adams
Henry Ford
Henry Frost
Henry James
Henry Jones Ford
Henry Seton Merriman
Henry W Longfellow
Herbert A. Giles
Herbert N. Casson
Herman Hesse
Homer
Honore De Balzac
Horace Walpole
Horatio Alger Jr.
Howard Pyle
Howard R. Garis
Hugh Lofting
Hugh Walpole
Humphry Ward
Ian Maclaren
Inez Haynes Gillmore
Irving Bacheller
Israel Abrahams
Ivan Turgenev
J.G.Austin

J. Henri Fabre
J. M. Barrie
J. Macdonald Oxley
J. S. Fletcher
J. S Knowles
J. Storer Clouston
Jack London
Jacob Abbott
James Allen
James Andrews
James Baldwin
James DeMille
James Joyce
James Lane Allen
James Lane Allen
James Cliver Curwood
James Oppenheim
James Otis
James R. Driscoll
Jane Austen
Janet Aldridge
Jens Peter Jacobsen
Jerome K. Jerome
John Burroughs
John Cournos
John F. Kennedy
John Gay
John Glasworthy
John Habberton
John Joy Bell
John Kendrick Bangs
John Milton
John Philip Sousa
Jonas Lauritz Idemil Lie
Jonathan Swift
Joseph A. Altsheler
Joseph Carey
Joseph Conrad
Joseph E. Badger Jr
Joseph Hergesheimer
Joseph Jacobs
Jules Vernes
Julian Hawthrone
Julie A Lippmann
Justin Huntly McCarthy
Kakuzo Okakura
Kenneth Grahame
Kenneth McGaffey
Kate Langley Bosher
Kate Langley Bosher
Katherine Cecil Thurston

Katherine Stokes
L. A. Abbot
L. T. Meade
L. Frank Baum
Latta Griswold
Laura Lee Hope
Laurence Housman
Lawrence Beasley
Leo Tolstoy
Leonid Andreyev
Lewis Carroll
Lewis Sperry Chafer
Lilian Bell
Lloyd Osbourne
Louis Hughes
Louis Tracy
Louisa May Alcott
Lucy Fitch Perkins
Lucy Maud Montgomery
Lydia Miller Middleton
Lyndon Orr
M. Corvus
M. H. Adams
Margaret E. Sangster
Margaret Vandercook
Margret Penrose
Maria Edgeworth
Maria Thompson Daviess
Mariano Azuela
Marion Polk Angellotti
Mark Overton
Mark Twain
Mary Austin
Mary Catherine Crowley
Mary Cole
Mary Hastings Bradley
Mary Roberts Rinehart
Mary Rowlandson
M. Wollstonecraft Shelley
Maud Lindsay
Max Beerbohm
Myra Kelly
Nathaniel Hawthrone
Nicolo Machiavelli
O. F. Walton
Oscar Wilde
Owen Johnson
P.G. Wodehouse
Paul and Mabel Thorne
Paul G. Tomlinson
Paul Severing

Percy Brebner
Peter B. Kyne
Plato
R. Derby Holmes
R. L. Stevenson
R. S. Ball
Rabindranath Tagore
Rahul Alvares
Ralph Bonehill
Ralph Henry Barbour
Ralph Victor
Ralph Waldo Emmerson
Rene Descartes
Rex Beach
Rex E. Beach
Richard Harding Davis
Richard Jefferies
Richard Le Gallienne
Robert Barr
Robert Frost
Robert Gordon Anderson
Robert L. Drake
Robert Lansing
Robert Lynd
Robert Michael Ballantyne
Robert W. Chambers
Rosa Nouchette Carey
Rudyard Kipling
Samuel B. Allison
Samuel Hopkins Adams
Sarah Bernhardt
Sarah C. Hallowell
Selma Lagerlof
Sherwood Anderson
Sigmund Freud
Standish O'Grady
Stanley Weyman
Stella Benson
Stephen Crane
Stewart Edward White
Stijn Streuvels
Swami Abhedananda
Swami Parmananda
T. S. Ackland
T. S. Arthur
The Princess Der Ling
Thomas A. Janvier
Thomas A Kempis
Thomas Anderton
Thomas Bailey Aldrich
Thomas Bulfinch
Thomas De Quincey
Thomas H. Huxley
Thomas Hardy
Thomas More
Thornton W. Burgess
U. S. Grant
Valentine Williams
Various Authors
Vaughan Kester
Victor Appleton
Virginia Woolf
Walter Camp
Walter Scott
Washington Irving
Wilbur Lawton
Wilkie Collins
Willa Cather
Willard F. Baker
William Dean Howells
William le Queux
W. Makepeace Thackeray
William W. Walter
Winston Churchill
Yei Theodora Ozaki
Yogi Ramacharaka
Young E. Allison
Zane Grey

www.ingramcontent.com/pod-product-compliance
Lightning Source LLC
Chambersburg PA
CBHW030329180626
46810CB00003B/1289